Alfred Lutschaunig

New Spanish and English nautical, maritime and technical dictionary

AF210497

Salzwasser

Alfred Lutschaunig

New Spanish and English nautical, maritime and technical dictionary

1. Auflage | ISBN: 978-3-84605-050-7

Erscheinungsort: Frankfurt, Deutschland

Erscheinungsjahr: 2020

Salzwasser Verlag GmbH

Reprint of the original, first published in 1869.

NEW

SPANISH AND ENGLISH

NAUTICAL, MARITIME & TECHNICAL

DICTIONARY,

CONTAINING NEARLY 6000 WORDS,

WITH ALL THE

EXPRESSIONS USED IN THE CONSTRUCTION
AND NAVIGATION OF VESSELS.

IN TWO PARTS:

I.—SPANISH AND ENGLISH.
II.—ENGLISH AND SPANISH.

COPYRIGHT ENTERED AT STATIONERS' HALL.

CAREFULLY COMPILED BY

ALFRED LUTSCHAUNIG.

LONDON: LONGMAN & CO. 39 PATERNOSTER ROW.
LIVERPOOL: ROCKLIFF BROTHERS, 44 CASTLE STREET.
1869.

DICCIONARIO NUEVO

DE LAS ESPRESIONES MAS USUALES EN LA

CONSTRUCCION Y NAVEGACION

DE BUQUES;

CONTENIENDO CERCA DE 6000 PALABRAS.

EN DOS PARTES:

I.—ESPAÑOL ó INGLES.
II.—INGLES y ESPAÑOL.

———

EL AUTOR SE RESERVA EL DERECHO DE REPRODUCCION
É IMPRENTA.

———

RECOPILADO CUIDADOSAMENTE POR

ALFRED LUTSCHAUNIG.

LÓNDRES: LONGMAN & CO. 39 PATERNOSTER ROW.
LIVERPOOL: ROCKLIFF BROTHERS, 44 CASTLE STREET.

1869.

PREFACE.

THE words and expressions of ordinary conversation are not such as are used in particular pursuits; and the words and expressions of one profession are hardly understood by those engaged in another. Each calling adopts its own peculiar mode and means of conveying the idea of its requirements. The nautical phraseology, in particular, has so many peculiar, original and characteristic phrases which are wholly incomprehensible to landsmen generally, that the casual translator of naval documents, though, in a measure, possessed of the languages he may be transposing, finds himself frequently at a loss to understand and properly interpret the expressions he meets.

The Editor, in his intercourse with seafaring men, has felt the serious inconvenience of having no book or dictionary, of easy reference, giving the peculiar meanings of the expressions and words used by them.

Having felt this want himself, he believes he has rendered a service to the Spanish Marine, and to Englishmen engaged with the Spanish shipping, and to all interpreters and translators of nautical documents, in English and Spanish, by having compiled the present book. He has consulted every known author in both tongues, and has drawn from all sources. He hopes, therefore, that his Nautical and Technical Dictionary of all the most usual terms will prove a valuable asssistance to any who may require it.

PRÓLOGO.

Por donde navegue el marino español, se encuentra frente á frente con la marina de Inglaterra, que con extraordinario desarrollo estiende su comercio sobre el orbe entero.

El conocimiento del idioma ingles ofrece grandes ventajas, y es casi indispensable, á todo viagéro en general, peró á nadie mas esencial que al marino. Sin embargo, un conocimiento general de la lengua, poco le valdría, puesto que las palabras y espresiones que son mas necesarias para él, son tecnicas y esclusivas á la marina; y en su mayor parte, desconocidas, aun de los mismos ingleses, que no son de aquella profesion. Hay una abundancia y profusion de estos terminos y espresiones, que en sí solos forman un lenguaje separado; y son bastantes para llenar un libro completo. El autor de esta obra, en su trato diario con hombres de mar de ambas naciones, á menudo, ha palpado la falta de un libro ó diccionario, en el cual, con facilidad, hallase los equivalentes exactos de las palabras y espresiones mas usuales, empleadas en la navegacion y construccion de buques, y en el comercio maritimo; y ha tenido que recojer estos informes con mucho trabajo y paciencia. Esta necesidad y vacío que se le ha presentado con tanta exigencia, le ha inducido á emprendér la recopilacion de este diccionario, que espéra será util á la marina española, y á todos los que tengan trato ó relaciones con ella. El autor ha recopilado cuidadosamente de los trabajos de todos los publicistas mas conocidos y de merito, añadiendo ó suprimiendo aquello que considera necesario ó superfluo, para no dificultar la comprension de su obra, fruto de su propia experencia.

Espéra, pues, que será acojido este trabajo, por los navegantes, navieros y constructores españoles, con la bondad que siempre saben dispensar á toda empresa útil, y la conviccion de haber contribuido á facilitar la comprension del idioma de mar, será para el autor sobrada recompensa.

DICCIONARIO NUEVO

DE LAS EXPRESIÓNES MAS USUÁLES EN LA

CONSTRUCCION Y NAVEGACION DE BUQUES

EN

ESPAÑOL É INGLES.

Aballestár, to haul a cable.

Abanico, a spritsail.

Abaníco (fóque de), concentrated jib.

Abarbetár, to lash, to seize.

Abarloár, to lay alongside, to bear up, to haul the wind.

Abarrotár, to fill up to the beams, to trim the hold.

Abarróte, a small package for filling up the cavities in the stowage of a cargo.

Abatimíento, leeway.

Abatír, to fall to leeward, to go adrift.

Abiérto, undecked, open.

Abitadúra, a turn of the cable around the bits.

Abítas del molinéte, carrick bits.

Abítar, to bite the cable, to fasten the cable to the bits.

Abitónes, topsailsheets, bits.

Abocár la artillería, to bring the guns to bear.

Abocár un estrécho, to enter the mouth of a channel.

Abonanzár, to calm, to clear up.

Abordáje, the act of boarding, the running foul of.

Abordár, to board.

B

Aboyár, to lay down buoys.

Abra, the spread.

Abrazár, to fathom.

Abromádo, dark, hazy, foggy.

Abromárse, to become worm-eaten.

Abrotonár, to scud a hull.

Acantiládo, easy of access (as applied to a coast).

Achúelas de abordáge, boarding axes.

Acolladór, lanyard.

Acolladóres de los obénques, lanyards of the shrouds.

Acorullár, to bridle the oars.

Acuartelár, to flat in a sail.

Aculebrár, to lace.

Adrizár, to right a ship.

Adúja, fake, coil.

Adujár, to coil a cable.

Afelpádos, cased mats.

Aferrár, to furl.

Aferrár, to serve, to ease.

Aferrár un cábo, to serve a rope.

Aferravélas, furling-lines, rope bands.

Afirmár, to haul up, to make fast.

Aflechátes, ratlines, or ratlings.

Aflojár los obénques, to ease the shrouds.

Afondár, to sink, to founder.

Agarradéro, anchoring ground.

Agolár, to hand the sails.

Aguáda (hacér), to provide a ship with water.

Aguáda, place where ships go to take in water.

Aguáje del timón, dead water, wake, rapid current
    of sea water.

Aguas, dead water, wake.

Aguas (buénas), in good trim, with proper draft of
    water.

Aguas (entre dos), between wind and water.

Aguas (muértas), neap tides.
Aguas (vivas), spring tides.
Agújas, sail needles.
Agúja de mareár, mariner's compass.
Agúja de cámara, hanging compass.
Alas, studdingsails.
Alas de gávia, main-topmast studdingsails.
Alas de velácho, fore-topmast studdingsails.
Alas de juanéte mayór, main-topgallant studdingsails.
Alas de sobremayór, main-royal studdingsails.
Alas de juanéte de próa, fore-topgallant studdingsails.
Alas de sobrejuanéte, royals studdingsails.
Alas de cangréja, ring tailsail.
Alas de mesána, driver.
Alacénas, lockers on board a ship.
Alár, to haul.
Alargár, to pay out, to sheer off.
Alastrár, to ballast.
Alcázar, quarter-deck.
Alétas, fashion pieces.
Alétas de una manguéra, goose-wings.
Alijerár, to lighten.
Alijár, to lighten.
Alíjo, the lightening of a ship, a lighter.
Aljíbe, cistern, floating cistern, watering-boat.
Aljíbes, tanks.
Alma, strengthening-line.
Almacén, water-butt on deck.
Almiránta, the admiral's ship.
Almirantázgo, the board of admiralty.
Almiránte, admiral.
Almogáma, the hindermost timber in the stern.
Almohadílla, buffer.
Alotár las ánclas, to stow the anchors.
Alquitrán, tar.

Alta mar, high seas.

Alteróso, high topped.

Aluár, ó tomar por la lúa, to bring by the lee.

Alunamiénto, the roaching.

Alunár, to roach.

Amánte, tye, runner, part of the running rigging.

Amánte de viradór, top-rope.

Amánte de rízos, reef-tackle.

Amántes, rúnners.

Amantillár, to top the lifts.

Amantíllo, lift.

Amantíllos de la botavára, topping-lifts.

Amárra, cable or moorings.

Amarradúra, the lashing, the seizing.

Amárras, fasts.

Amárras fijas, moorings.

Amárras de pópa, stern-posts.

Amárras de próa, head-fasts.

Amárras de través, breast-fasts.

Amarrazónes, groundtackle.

Amoldár, to crease.

Amollár, to keep away, to ease off.

Amortiguár, to deaden, to lessen.

Amúra, tack, bow, luff.

Amúra de la mayór, main-tack.

Amúra del trinquéte, fore-tack.

Amúra á babór, larboard tack.

Amúra á estribór, starboard tack.

Amúra (cambiár la), to stand on the other tack.

Amúra de revés, leeward tack.

Amúra de uña bandéra, tack of a flag.

Amúra (por la), on the bow.

Amuráda, side.

Amurádas, spirketing or spirket-rising.

Amurár, to haul on board the tack.

Amurár la mayór, to haul on board the main-tack.
Anca, the quarter.
Ancla, anchor.
Ancla del ayúste, ó de úso, best bower.
Ancla del creciénte, flood anchor.
Ancla de esperánza, sheet anchor.
Ancla de már, sea anchor.
Ancla de la pláya, shore anchor.
Ancla del menguánte, ebb anchor.
Ancla sencílla, ó de levá, small anchor.
Ancla de servidúmbre, bower anchor.
Ancláje, anchorage.
Anclóte, stream-anchor, grapnel.
Andár (el), the headway, the sailing, the speed.
Andár en buéna véla, to keep the sail full.
Andár todo, to bear up the helm.
Andadór, a fast sailer.
Andána, tier or row of guns.
Andanáda, broadside, volley.
Andarivél, girtline.
Anegádo, water-logged.
Anemómetro, Anemometer (an instrument by which
    the pressure of the wind on a given surface is
    ascertained.)
Anguílas, slips for launching ships.
Aníllo, grommet.
Antagálla, balance reef, sprit-sail, reef-bands.
Antagallár, to balance.
Anténa, a lateen yard.
Anzuélo, fish-hook.
Apágapenól, leech-line, leech-rope.
Apagavéla, spilling-line.
Aparejadór, rigger.
Aparejár, to rig, to fit.
Aparéjo, tackle, burton, rigging on board a ship.

Aparéjo de amánte y estrélla, runner-tackle.
Aparéjo de cómbes, luff-tackle.
Aparéjo de estríque, garnet-tackle.
Aparéjo redóndo, ó de crúz, square rigged.
Aparéjo latíno, lateen rig.
Aparéjo de amúra, tack-tackle.
Aparéjo de estrelléras de cómbes, winding-tackle.
Aparéjo de estríque, garnet, tackle for lowering and
    hoisting goods in and out of the hold.
Aparéjo de viradór, top-tackle.
Aparéjo de peñól, yard-tackle.
Aparéjo de pescánte, fish-tackle.
Aparéjo principál, main and topsails.
Aparéjo mayór, after-sails.
Aparéjo de poléa, burton.
Aparéjo de próa, head-sails.
Aparéjo lárgo, all sails out.
Aparéjo de bolína, tacking trim.
Aparéjo de bolineár, bowline-tackle.
Aparéjo lléno, to keep full.
Aparéjo réal, winding-tackle, main-tackle.
Aparéjo de viradór, top-tackle.
Aparéjo de rolín, rolling-tackle.
Aparéjo de gáta, cat-tackle.
Aparéjo del tércio de las vérgas mayóres, quarter-
    tackle.
Aparejuélos, small tackles.
Aparejuélos de pórtas, port-tackles.
Aparejuélos de rízos, reef-tackles.
Aparejuélos de socaíre, jigger-tackles.
Apopádo, trimmed by the stern.
Aproádo, trimmed by the head.
Aproár, to turn the head of a ship towards any part.
Aproár al viénto, to come to the wind.
Apuntár, to stitch.

Apuntalár, to prop or shore a vessel.

Aráña, crowfoot.

Arandélas, washers.

Arca de fuégo, fire-chest, a small box filled with gunpowder, pebbles and nails, used to annoy an enemy attempting to board a ship.

Arrancár el áncla, drag the anchor.

Arboladúra, masting, masts and spars, rigging.

Arbolár, to mast.

Arbolánte de pié de campána, bell-crank, or where the bell is hung.

Arfáda, pitching of a ship.

Arfár, to pitch, longitudinal movement of a ship.

Argána, ó Argólla, anchor-ring, ring-bolt.

Armadór, shipowner, ship's husband.

Armáda, a fleet, a squadron, armada.

Armádo de barlovénto, the fleet stationed to windward.

Armadéra, principal timbers of a ship.

Armaménto, equipment, fitting out.

Armár, to fit out, to equip, to arm, to man a ship

Armazón, frame of a ship.

Aros, cringles.

Arpéo, grappling iron.

Arpón, harpoon.

Arqueár, to measure, to survey a ship, to take the tonnage.

Arraigádo, standing part of a rope, foot-hook shrouds.

Arrancáda, the start, the head-way.

Arranchár, to trim down a sheet.

Arrastráculo, water-sail.

Arrastradéro, a careening place.

Arriár, to draw down, to heave down, to ease, to strike, to slack up.

Arriár en bánda, to let go a-main, to pay out the whole cable.

Arriár la bandéra, to strike the colors.

Arriár las vérgas y los masteléros, to strike the yards and topmasts.

Arriár un cabo, to pay out a cable.

Arríba, up, aloft.

Arribáda, falling off, the calling in, or touching at a port in distress, the arrival of a vessel.

Arribár, to bear away, to bear down, to turn away, to fall off from the wind, to bear up, to put into a port in distress.

Arribár en redóndo, to fly up.

Arribár á la bánda, hard a-weather.

Arribár todo, to bear away before the wind.

Arribár á escóte lárgo, to bear away large.

Arribár sobre un bajél, to bear down upon a ship.

Arrimár, to moor close to any place.

Arrizár, to reef.

Arranzár, to drive.

Arrúfo ó Arrufadúra, sheer, sheerwall, rise, saddle, gauging.

Arrumáge, stowage of a ship's cargo.

Arrumár, to stow a cargo.

Arrumazón, the act and effect of stowing, an overcast horizon.

Arrumbár, to resume and steer the proper course.

Arza, fall of a tackle.

Aspa, cross-gore.

Asta, staff, sprit.

Asta de bandéra de pópa, ensign-staff.

Asta de bandéra de próa, jackstaff.

Asta de tope, flagstaff.

Astílla muérta, the rising, the dead rising of the floor timbers.

Astilléro, stocks, shipwrights' yard, dockyard.

Atormentár, to strain, to stress.

Atortorár, to lash with twisting, to strengthen the hull.

Atravesárse, to lie to, to lie by, to set athwart.

Aurica, bermudoe sail.

Avería, damage, average, stress.

Avería gruésa, general average.

Avíso, advice boat.

Ayustár, to fast, to splice, to bend two ropes.

Ayúste, the bend, the fast of two ropes.

Ayúda de cocinéro, the cook's shifter.

Ayúda de dispenséro, the steward's mate.

Ayúda de viradór, a false preventer.

Azafrán del timon, afterpiece of the rudder.

Azafrán del tajamár, forepiece of the cutwater.

Azorádo (navio), a badly stowed ship, sailing heavily.

B

Babór, port, larboard, left-hand side of a ship standing with the face towards the head.

Babór (á, por, de) to port.

Babór (de babór á estribór,) athwart ship.

Babór todo (á), head a-port.

Badázas, keys of the bonnets.

Bajél, general name for all ships, barges, lighters, boats.

Bajél desaparejádo, a ship unrigged.

Bajél boyánte, a light ship.

Bajél de bájo bórdo, a low-built ship.

Bajeléro, owner or master of a vessel.

Baibén, rattling line.

Balánce, rolling of a ship.

Balanceadór, a heavy roller.

Balancéla, an Italian fishing boat.
Balándra, cutter, sloop.
Baldeár, to throw water with buckets.
Balísa, buoy.
Balón, a state vessel in Siam.
Bálsa, a raft or float.
Balsílla, a small raft.
Bancáda, thwart, seat of a rower.
Bánda, side.
Bánda (á la), heeled or hove down.
Bánda (arriár en), to let go a-main.
Bánda (dár en), to heel.
Bándas del tajamár, the cheeks of the head.
Bánda (en,) slack, untight, a-main.
Bandéra, flag, banner, standard.
Bandéra cuádra ó de insígnia, flag officer.
Bandéra de guérra, national flag.
Bandéra mercánte, merchant flag.
Bandéra de gála, great ensign.
Bandéra de próa, jack.
Bandéra de señáles, signal flag.
Bandéra blanca, the flag of truce.
Banderéta, a small flag, banneret, or bannerol.
Bandóla, a jurymast.
Báo, beam.
Báo maéstro, midship-beam.
Báos del sollado, orlop beams.
Báos de las cubiértas altas, the beams of the upper
    deck.
Báos del saltíllo de próa, forecastle beams.
Báos y crucétas de los pálos, cross and trestle trees.
Barbéta, lashing, rack-line, ring-rope.
Barbiquéjo, bob-stay.
Bárca, barque, boat, barge.
Bárca cháta, flat-bottomed boat.

Barcalónga, a fishing boat.
Barcáza, a large ferry boat.
Barcázo, a large barge.
Bárco, any sort of vessel.
Barcolóngo, an oblong boat with a round head.
Barcón, a large boat.
Bardágo, loof-hook rope.
Barloár, to lay alongside, to grapple for the purpose
   of boarding.
Barlóas, relieving-tackle, or relieving-tackle pendants.
Barloventeár, to work to windward, beating to wind-
   ward, to weather.
Barloventeár, to ply to windward, to beat about.
Barlovénto, weather-gauge, the point from whence
   the wind blows.
Barlovénto (costa de), the weather shore.
Barlovénto (costado de), the weather side.
Barlovénto (ganár el), to get to windward, to gain
   the wind.
Barquílla, little boat, wherry.
Barquílla de la corredéra, triangular piece of wood
   fastened to the log-line.
Bárra, crow-bar.
Bárras de cabrestánte y molinéte, the bars of the
   capstan and windlass.
Bárras de escotíllas, bars of the hatches.
Bárras de portas, gun-port bars.
Barraganéte, top timber, bulwark stanchions.
Barredéras, studdingsails.
Barrenadór, auger, or borer.
Barrenár un navío ó dár barréno, to sink a ship.
Barrér un navío de pópa á próa, to rake a ship fore
   and aft.
Barríga, bunt, belly.
Barriléte, mouse.

Barriléte de estái, the mouse of a stay.
Barriléte de rémo, the mouse of an oar.
Barrótes, battens.
Barrótes de las escotíllas, battens of the hatches.
Barrotínes de los báos, carlings, or carlines.
Barrotínes ó báos de la toldílla, carline-knees, or the beams of the stern.
Bastárdo de un racaménto, parrel-rope.
Bastidór, frame for canvass bulkheads.
Bastiménto, vessel (Italian word).
Batafiól, gasket.
Batallól, jib-boom.
Batayóla, bulwark, hammock rail.
Batayólas de los empalletádos, quarter-netting rails.
Batayólas de las cófas, toprails.
Batayólas del pasamáno, gangway rails.
Batículo, mizen.
Batidéro, toplining, top-cloth.
Batidéro, wash-board.
Batidéro de una véla, foot-tabling of a sail.
Batidéro de próa, wash-board of the cutwater.
Batidór, strengthening-line.
Batiénte de la bandéra, fly of an ensign.
Batiénte de un díque, apron of a dock.
Batiportár, to house a gun on board a ship.
Batír bandéras, to salute with the colors.
Bauprés, bowsprit.
Báza, ouzy ground.
Béque, head of the ship, privies for the sailors in the head grating.
Bergantín, brig.
Bergantínbarca, barque.
Bergantinéjo, small brig.
Bergantín goléta, schooner brig-rigged forward.
Berlínga, round timber of six inches in diameter.

Bertéllo, truck, bull's eye.

Bertéllo de canál, channel-truck.

Besár (á), home, close home, to touch.

Béta, line, rope, hawser laid rope.

Béta blánca, untarred line, white rope.

Béta négra ó alquitranáda, tarred line.

Betún, stuff with which the masts and bottoms of ships are payed.

Biáje, slope, slopewise.

Bichéro, boat-hook.

Bichéro (ásta de), the shaft of a boat-hook.

Bichéro (gáncho de), the hook of a boat-hook.

Bigorrílla, round seam.

Bigóta, dead-eye.

Bilórta, burr, a sort of iron ring used for various purposes on board a ship.

Binatéras, beckets, strops or ends of ropes.

Biquitórtes, quarter-gallery knees.

Biráda, tack.

Biráda de bórdo, the act of putting the ship about.

Birár, to wind, to twist, to tack, to go about.

Birár el cabrestánte, to heave at the capstan.

Birár para próa, to heave a-head.

Birár para pópa, to heave a-stern.

Birár el cáble, to heave taut.

Birár de bórdo, to tack or go about.

Birár de bórdo tomándo por avánte, to put the ship to windward.

Birár de bórdo en redóndo, to put the ship to leeward.

Birar por las águas de otro bajél, to tack in the wake of another ship.

Bira, bira, heave cheerily.

Biságras de la portéria, port-hinges.

Bitácora, binnacle or bittacle, compass-box.

Bitácora (lámpara de la), a binnacle lamp.

Bitacora (cuadérno de), log-book.
Bitadúra, cable-bit.
Bitadúra entéra de cáble, weather-bit of a cable.
Bitadúra (tomár la bitadúra con el cáble), to bit the
    cable.
Bítas, bits or bitts.
Bítas (ferro de las), lining of the bits.
Bítas (contra), standards of the bits.
Bítas de molinéte, windlass bitts.
Bitónes, pins of the capstan.
Blandáles, the maintop backstays.
Bloquéo, blockade of a port.
Bóca, throat.
Bóca de botavára, throat of the main-boom.
Bóca de lóbo, lubber's hole.
Bóca de finája, holes in the caps to allow the masts
    to pass.
Bóca de lóbo del tamboréte, caphole for the topmast.
Bóca de la escotilla, hatchway.
Bodéga, the hold.
Bodéga de pópa, after-hold.
Bodéga de próa, fore-hold.
Bogadór, rower.
Bogár, to pull, to row.
Bogár á cuartéles, to row by divisions.
Bojár, to sail round an island or cape.
Bolíche, foretopsail-bowline.
Bolína de barlovénto, weather bowline.
Bolína de trinquéte, fore-bowline.
Bolína (dar un salto á la), to ease or check the bowline.
Bolína (presentár la), to snatch the bowline.
Bolína (navegár de), to sail with bowlines hauled.
Bolína (ir á la bolína), to sail with a side wind.
Bolína, bowline.
Bolína de revés, lee bowline.

Bolínas de hamáca, hammock crowfoot.

Bolinéro, good plier.

Bolineár, to haul up the bowline in light winds.

Bolinéte, a movable capstan on the deck, in which the whipstaff moves.

Bolónes, square bolts or mortar-bed pintles, which serve to fasten the cheeks to the bed.

Bólsos, belly of a sail.

Bómba, pump.

Bombárda, bombarder.

Bonánza, fair weather.

Bonéta, bonnet, drabler.

Bórda, gunwale.

Bórdada, board, tack.

Bordáje, side planks of a ship.

Bórdo, board.

Bórdo, side, ship's outside.

Bórdo (á), aboard, on board.

Bórdo á la tiérra, to stand in-shore.

Bórdo á la mar, to stand off.

Bórdos (dár), to tack.

Borneadéro, berth of a ship at anchor.

Borneár, to bend, turn or twist.

Borneár (el navío bornéa), the ship swings round her anchor.

Bóta, water-cask.

Botadór, starting-pole (used to shove off a boat from the shore.)

Botalón, boom.

Botalón de fóque, jibboom.

Botalón de petifóque, flying-jibboom.

Botalón rastréro, swing-boom.

Botalónes de ála, stud-boom, studdingsail-booms.

Botántes, shores, outriggers.

Botár al água, to launch.

Botavánte, a pike used as a defensive arm by seamen.
Botavára, main-boom, driver-boom, outrigger.
Botavára de cangréja, gaffsail-boom
Bóte, boat.
Bóte (primér), pinnace.
Bóte (segúndo), cutter.
Bóte (tercér), yawl.
Bóte (cuárto), jolly-boat.
Bóte de pasáje, wherry, ferry-boat.
Bóte láncha, longboat.
Botequín, cog, small boat.
Boyár, a kind of Flemish bilander.
Boya, buoy.
Bóza, boat-rope, painter.
Bózas de la uña del áncla, shank-painter.
Bózas de cáble, cable stoppers.
Bózas de las vérgas, the stoppers of the yards.
Bózas de los obénques, the stoppers of the shrouds.
Braceár, to brace.
Braceár á ceñír, to brace or trim sharp up, to trim
    up by the wind.
Braceár en crúz, to square the yards.
Braceár en viénto, to fill the sails.
Braceár en fácha, to back the sails, to set aback.
Braceár al fílo, to spill, to shiver a sail.
Braceár en cája, to brace sharp up.
Bracéo, bracing.
Bragáda, the throat of a knee.
Bragáda (madéra de), compass-timber.
Braguéro, bunt.
Braguéro de cañón, breaching of a gun.
Braguéro de una véla, bunt of a sail.
Brandál, back-stay.
Brandáles de masteléro de gávia, the maintop-back-
    stays.

Brandáles volántes, shifting backstays.
Bráva (már), very rough sea.
Brázas, braces tied to the yards.
Bráza de la mayór, main-brace.
Brázas de barlovénto, weather-braces.
Brázas de sotavénto, lee-braces.
Brázas de la cebadéra, spritsail-braces.
Brázas (halár sóbre las), to haul in the braces.
Brazáge, depth of water, number of fathoms.
Brazál, rail.
Brazáles de próa, headrails.
Brazál del médio de próa, the middle rail of the head.
Brazalétes, brace pendants.
Brazólas, frames, combings of the hatchways.
Bréa, pitch.
Brín, combings of hemp.
Brinéte, light canvas.
Bringabála, brake or handle of a pump.
Brióles, brails.
Brióles del pujámen, bunt-lines.
Briólin, spilling-line, slab-line.
Bróma, wood borer, ship piercer, a worm which
    perforates the bottoms of ships.
Bromádo, worm-eaten; applied to the bottom of a
    ship damaged by wood-borers.
Brújula, sea-compass.
Brulóte, a fire-ship, a vessel loaded with combustible
    matter intended to set others on fire.
Brúsca, gore, bevel, sweep, rounding of masts, etc.
Brúsca totál, total amount of the gore.
Brúsca de costúra, eating in seaming.
Brúsca de pujámen, foot-gore.
Brúsca de cuchíllo, leech-gore.
Brúsca del grátil, stay-gore.
Brúsca de la caída de próa, mast-gore,

Brúsca del martíllo, tack-gore.
Brúsca de revés, reversed-gore.
Bucosidád, tonnage, burthen, bulk or capacity of a ship.
Búque, ship, vessel.
Búque en rósca, hull, hulk of a ship.
Búque de guérra, man-of-war.
Búque mercánte, merchantman.
Búque redóndo, cuádro ó de crúz, square-rigged vessel.
Búque latíno, lateen-rigged vessel.
Búque de véla, sailing ship or vessel.
Búque de vapór, steamer.
Búque místo, steam and sailing vessel.
Búque de travesía, out-bound ship, long-course ship.
Búque de cabotáge, coaster, small craft.
Búque ceñído, close-hauled ship.
Búque rancéro, a leeward ship.
Búque marinéro, a good sailer.
Búque tormentóso, a laboursome ship.
Búque pesádo, a slow, slack, heavy sailer.
Búque fálso ó celóso, a cranky ship.
Búque dúro, a stiff ship.
Búque de múchos llénos, a bluff-bowed ship.
Búque de múchos delgádos, a sharp-bottomed ship.
Búque veléro, a fast sailing ship.
Búque cargádo, a laden ship.
Búque de múcha guínda, a taunt or overmasted ship.
Búque abiérto de bócas, falling-home vessel, tumbling-
    sided ship.
Búque de cubiérta corrída, a decked vessel, a flush-
    decked ship.
Búque de toldílla, a poop-decked ship.
Burél, driving fid, splicing fid, setting fid.
Buréles de hiérro para engarzár motónes, splicing fids.
Busárdas, breast-hooks, compass-timbers.

C

Cabáco, end of a round timber which remains when masts are made.

Caballéte, rope-laying trussel, a stake head.

Cabeceadór, pitching ship.

Cabeceár, to pitch.

Cabéza, head, the fore part of a vessel.

Cabéza del búque, head.

Cabezáda, the pitching of a ship.

Cabílla, wooden pin for the fastening of the outside planking, belaying-pins.

Cabilléro, range of belaying pins, pin-rack.

Cáble, cable.

Cáble de esperánza, sheet-cable, largest on board ship.

Cáble del ayúste, best bower cable.

Cáble sencíllo ó de léva, small bower cable.

Cábo, rope, line.

Cábo blánco, untarred rope.

Cábo de labór, running rope.

Cábo (dár), to throw out rope.

Cabotáje, coasting trade, pilotage.

Cabrestánte, capstan or capstern.

Cabullería, cordage, ropes.

Cachéte, bow, cheek of a ship.

Cachólas, hounds, cheeks of the masts.

Cachópo, gulf of the sea between rocks.

Cadéna, chain.

Cadéna de rócas, ledge of rocks.

Caér á sotavénto, to drive to leeward.

Cágue, kaag, a Dutch vessel with one mast, a kind of bilander.

Caída, the hoist.

Caída al céntro, drop, hoist in the middle.

Caída de fuéra, depth, drop, outer leech.
Caída de déntro, inner leech.
Caída de una bandéra, standing part of a flag.
Caída de pálo, rake.
Caída del búque, casting, falling-off of a ship.
Caída de próa, casting or falling-off.
Caída de una véla, depth or drop of a sail.
Caíque, caic, a kind of skiff or small boat.
Cája de água, manger of a ship.
Cája de bómbas, pump-well of a ship.
Cája de lástre, ballast-case.
Cája de már, sea-chest.
Cája (metér las vérgas en), to place the yards in a
       horizontal position.
Cajéra, sheave-hole.
Cajéta, sennit, fox, caburn.
Cála, a creek or small bay.
Calabróte, cablet, stream cable.
Caládo, draught of water of a vessel.
Caládo de un pálo, housing of a mast.
Calcés, mast-head.
Caladór, caulking-iron.
Calafáte, caulker.
Calafateár, to caulk, or fill up the seams of a ship
       with oakum and pitch.
Calalúz, a kind of East Indian vessel.
Calár el timón, to hang the rudder.
Calár el pálo de un navío, to step a mast.
Calár tántos piés, to draw so many feet of water.
Caldéro de bréa, pitch kettle.
Caldéro del equipáge, mess-kettle.
Caléta, creek, cove, a small bay or inlet.
Callejón de combáte, orlop-gangway.
Cálma, calm, smooth sea.
Cálma muérta ó cháta, dead calm.

Calóma, the singing-out of sailors when they haul a rope.

Calzár el áncla, to shoe the anchor.

Cámara, cabin.

Camaróte, room on board a ship, berth.

Camatónes, iron fastenings by which the shrouds are attached to a ship's sides.

Camíno, ship's way, rate of sailing.

Camiséta, bunt of a sail, skin.

Campáña, sea voyage, cruise.

Campáña (víveres de), sea provisions, stores.

Canál, channel, or narrow sea between two countries.

Canál de un brulóte, train-trough of a fire-ship.

Canário, a kind of barge used in the Canary Islands.

Cáncamo, ring-bolt.

Cáncamos de gáncho, hook-bolts.

Cáncamos de ójo, eye-bolts.

Candeléro de ójo, eye-stanchion or iron stay with ring.

Candeléro ciégo, blind-stanchion, or iron stay without a ring.

Candeléros del tóldo, awning stanchions.

Candeléros de portalónes, entering-rope stanchions.

Candeléros de trinchéras y parapétos, quarter-netting stanchions.

Candelízas, brails.

Candéla (en), upright.

Candeléros, crotches or stanchions.

Candelízas de barlovénto, weather-braces.

Candelízas de sotavénto, lee-braces.

Candelízas (cargár las mayóres sóbre las), to brail up the courses.

Candónga, ringtail.

Cangréja, bermudoe sail, boomsail, brigsail or gaffsail.

Cangréja mayór, main-sail.

Cangréjos, main and fore-trysail.

Canóa, yawl, gig.
Cantár el gobiérno del timón, to order the steersman how to steer the ship.
Cantéles, ends of old ropes put under the casks on board a ship to make them lie fast.
Cantimarónes, kind of boats.
Cáña, tiller, yoke.
Cáña del timón, tiller.
Cáñamo, hemp.
Cáñas de cebadéra, sprit-sail sheet-blocks.
Cañón de próa, bow-chase.
Cápa (á la), lying-to, trying.
Cápa del timón, rudder-coat.
Cápa de fogonadúras, mast-coat.
Cápa y sombréro, hat-money, primage.
Capacidád, bulk or burthen of a ship, tonnage.
Capcés, lateen mast-head.
Capeár, to try, to lie-to, to lie under the sea.
Caperól, head of stem.
Caperúza de fogón, hood of the caboose.
Caperúza de pálo, hood of a mast-head when the ship is unrigged.
Capíllo, cap, hood.
Capitán, captain.
Capitán de bandéra, captain of the admiral's ship.
Capitán de fragáta, captain of a frigate, post-captain.
Capitán de puérto, port-captain.
Capitán del puerto, harbour-master, water-bailiff.
Capón, anchor-stopper at the cat-head.
Capóta, coat, covering hood, any case of sail-cloth.
Capóte, storm-coat.
Capuchíno, corner.
Capuchínas, crotches and knees.
Cár, lower end of a lateen yard, weather arm.
Cára de pópa, aft-side, aft-part.

Carába, kind of vessel used in the Archipelago.
Carabéla, caravel, a long three-masted vessel.
Carabelón, brig or brigantine.
Carbonéra, main-staysail.
Carbonéro, collier, coal vessel.
Cárda, small vessel of peculiar build.
Caréna, careening or repairing of a ship.
Carenár (aparéjo de), careening gear.
Cárga, goods for shipment, cargo.
Cárga de péso, goods taken by weight.
Cárga de medída, goods taken by measurement,
    40 cubic feet to the ton.
Cargadéra, down-hauls, brails.
Cargaménto, cargo, freight of a ship.
Cargadéra, de una véla de estái, down-haul of a staysail.
Cargadéros de las gúvias, topsail brails.
Cargadéros (aparéjo de cargadéro de racaménto),
    down-haul tackle.
Cargadéro, place where goods are shipped or unshipped.
Cargadór, tackle.
Cargár, to load.
Cargár á fléte, to ship goods on freight.
Cargár arriba una véla. to clue up a sail.
Cargazón de tiémpo, thick cloudy weather.
Carlínga, carling.
Carróza, hood, awning, tarpaulin, small cabin of
    tarred boards.
Carracón, merchant ship of the largest size.
Carrillár, to hoist light things out of the hold of a
    vessel by means of tackle.
Carríllo, light hoisting-tackle.
Cartél, cartel-ship or flag of truce.
Cataviénto, vane, dog-vane, feather-vane.
Cátre, frame, cot-bottom.
Cascarója, ship-worm, wood-borer, ship-piercer.

Cascarrón, an old tub of a vessel, a sea-bruiser.
Cásco, hull, body, shell of the ship.
Castañuélas, cleats.
Castañuélas de pontón, ponton-cleats.
Castíllo, forecastle.
Catábre, sheep-shank.
Catúres, a kind of armed vessel of Bantam.
Cavílla, wooden pin for fastening the outside planking.
Cavillár, tree-nail, wooden pin, belaying-pin.
Cayúco, a small fishing-boat used in America.
Cazár, (dár cáza), to give chase, to chase, to pursue.
Cáza escóta, out-rigger, mizen-boom.
Cazár, to haul home, to sheet, to trim a sheet.
Cazár á besár, to sheet home.
Cazár una véla, to tally a sail, to haul the sheet aft.
Cazonéte, toggle.
Cebadéra, sprit-sail whisker.
Cegár una vía de água, to stop a leak.
Ceguiñéla, whip-staff of the helm.
Célda, small cabin on board a ship.
Cenéfas, valances, curtains, awnings.
Cenéfa de un tóldo, centre of an awning.
Ceñír, to luff, to haul the wind, to sail by the wind,
　　to touch the wind, to sail clue.
Cépo del áncla, anchor-stock.
Cépo de maniguétes, cross-piece of the kevil.
Cépo de molinéte, main piece of the windlass.
Cerrár, to master a sail, to lash up.
Cerviólas, catheads.
Chafaldéte, clue-line.
Chalána, lighter.
Chapaléta, part of a ship's pump, a valve.
Chapalétas de los imbornáles, the clappers of the
　　scupper-holes.
Chapúces, mast spars.

Charánchas, battens used as supporters on board ship.

Cháta, a flat-bottomed boat.

Cháta alijadóra, lighter.

Cháta de arbolár, sheer hulk.

Cháta de carenár, careening hulk.

Cháza, between-ports.

Chicóte, end or point of a rope.

Chicóte (de chicóte á chicóte), end-for-end.

Chífle, tide.

Chífles (águas), neap-tides.

Chiléra, row-lock-hole.

Chimenéa, funnel, chimney.

Chumacéra, cloth put on the side of a boat to prevent the oars from wearing it.

Chúzo, a kind of pike used on board ship as a defensive weapon.

Ciár, to back a-stern, to hold water.

Ciguéña, a laying-hook or winch.

Cimbornáles, scupper-holes.

Címbra, the bending of a board.

Cingladúra, a day's run or sailing, a watch of 4 hours.

Cinglár, to sail with a fair wind and full sails.

Clarabóya, skylight.

Cláva, scupper, or scupper-hole.

Clavazón, assortment of nails for shipbuilding.

Clávo, a nail.

Clóque, grapnel, harpoon.

Cóca, a sort of small vessel, turn or twist of a cable.

Cóche, a kind of coasting barge.

Cochináta, rider, timber for strengthening a vessel.

Cócle, a grapnel, grappling-iron in warfare.

Codáste, stern-post.

Codéra, a spring on a cable.

Cófa, top.

Coí, hammock.

Cóla de páto, rounding of the foot, sweep of the foot.

Cólcha ó Colchadúra, laying or twisting ropes.

Cómbes, waist of a ship.

Cómitre, boatswain on board a galley.

Compás de már ó brújula, mariner's compass.

Compasár una cárta de mareár, to mark the ship's course on the chart.

Compuérta de maréa, tide-gate.

Cónchas de escobénes, naval woods, pieces fitted into the hawse-holes to preserve the cable.

Conocimiénto, bill of lading.

Constrúccion de vélas, sail-making.

Contadór, purser.

Contrabráza, preventer-brace.

Contracuchillos, reversed goring-cloths.

Contradúza, second-halliard.

Contradurmiénte, clamp, thick stuff fastened to the inner part of a ship's side.

Contraestái, preventer-stay, spring-stay.

Contraempuñadúra, preventer-earing.

Contraescóta, preventer-sheet.

Contraescotín, preventer-topsail-sheet.

Contraestái del mayór ó del trinquéte, preventer-stay of the main or fore-mast.

Contraestambór, a knee which fastens the sternpost to the keel.

Contrafóque, fore-topmast-staysail, or flying-jib of a smack.

Contrahójas de las ventánas, dead lights of the cabin.

Contramaéstre, boatswain.

Contramaréa, counter-tide, spring-tide.

Contrapalanquín, preventer-clew-garnet.

Contraquílla, false keel.

Contraracaménto, preventer-parrel.

Contraróa ó Contraróda, stemson.

Contratrancaníles, inner water-ways.

Contráste, sudden change in the wind.

Contravolínas, brails.

Contrayúgo, inner transom.

Copón, a thick rope for weighing up the anchor.

Coracéro (búque), an iron-clad vessel.

Corál, a large knee which fastens the sternpost to the keel.

Corbatón, a small knee used in different parts of a ship.

Corbéta ó Corvéta, sloop, corvette.

Córcha, twisting.

Corchár, to lay, to twist.

Cordáje, cordage, ropes of the rigging.

Cordél, a thin rope.

Cordél de corredéra, log-line.

Cordón, strand of a cable or rope.

Cornamúsa, belaying cleat.

Cornamúsas de los pálos, the belaying-cleats of the lower masts.

Cornamúsas de pontón, the notched cleats of a ponton.

Córnas, backstays.

Cornéta, broad pendant, a rear-admiral's flag.

Coróna, pendant, span for launching ships.

Coronamiénto, taffrail or taffarel.

Corónas de los pálos, main-tackle pendants.

Corónas de quináles, preventer-shroud pendants.

Corrál, place for stowing cattle on board ship.

Corredór, gangway, balcony or stern-gallery.

Córso, a cruise.

Corredéra, log-line.

Corredéra (hechár la), to heave the lead.

Corredéra (corretél de la), log-reel.

Corretáje, brokerage.

Corrér, to run before the wind, to be under bare poles.

Corrér á la bolína ó trínca, to run close upon the wind.

Corrér del ótro bórdo, to stand on the other tack.
Corrér por bórdos ó bordeár, to ply to windward.
Corrér a dos púños, to run before the wind.
Corrér sobre un bajél, to chase a vessel.
Córsa, a coasting voyage, a cruise.
Corsário, privateer.
Cosér, to reeve, to lace, to lash.
Cosedéros de los tablónes, plank-seams.
Cosidúra, reeving, lashing.
Costádo, side of the vessel.
Cósta, the coast.
Cósta (navegár á la), to sail along the coast.
Costádo (navío de costádo derécho), a wall-sided ship.
Costádo (navío de costádo fálso), a lap-sided ship.
Costádo (dár el costádo al navío), to heave down a ship.
Costanéro ó Costeadór, a coasting vessel.
Costeár, to sail close to the coast.
Costéro, coaster.
Costíllas, ribs of a ship.
Costilláge, the frame of a ship, the timbers.
Costúra, splicing of a rope.
Costúras de los tablónes de un navío, the seams of
    the planks of a ship.
Costúras abiértas, open seams of a ship.
Cóte, half-hitch.
Cóy, hammock.
Cóz, heel of a mast.
Creciénte de la maréa, flood-tide.
Crucéro, cruising station.
Crúces, preventer-leech-lines of the topsails.
Crucétas, topgallant-mast crosstrees.
Crucétas de la cófa, crosstrees.
Crujía, the waist, the midship gangway.
Cruzámen, length of a yard.
Cruzámen de una véla, width of a sail.

Cruzár, to cruise.

Crúz de las bítas, crosspiece of the bits.

Crúz y botón, the frapping, crossing and joining parts of the tackle.

Crúz (braceár en), to square the yards.

Crúz (la), stern-frame.

Cuadérna maéstra, midship-bend or frame.

Cuadernál, block.

Cuadernál ciégo, heart, dead-block.

Cuadérna, the frame of a ship.

Cuadérna del cuérpo popés, stern-frame.

Cuadérnas de henchimiénto, filling-timbers.

Cuadérnas de la amúra, loof-frames.

Cuadérnas revirádas, cant-timber.

Cuadérnas á escuádra, square timbers.

Cuadernáles de carenár, careening gear.

Cuadernaléte, short double block.

Cuádra, square, quarter of a ship.

Cuádra (á la, por la), on the beam, on the quarter.

Cuaranténa, quarantine or quarantain.

Cuartél, hatch, the lid of a hatchway.

Cuárta, quarter, point of a compass.

Cubéta para alquitrán, tar-bucket.

Cubichéte, hood, hatch, water-board, weather-board.

Cubiérta, deck.

Cubiérta priméra ó principál, the main or gun deck.

Cubiérta (segúnda), middle-deck.

Cubiérta (tercéra), lower-deck.

Cubiérta del solládo, orlop.

Cubiérta entéra, flush deck.

Cubiérta arqueáda, a cambering deck.

Cubiérta cortáda, a cut or open deck.

Cuchárros ó Cucárros, harpings.

Cuchára para bréa, pitch-ladle.

Cuchárros (tablónes de), serving-planks,

Cuchíllo, leech.
Cuchíllos, goring-cloth.
Cuérdas de las cubiértas, deck-streaks, clamps.
Cuérpo del cabrestánte, barrel of a capstan.
Culádas, shocks and rollings of a ship.
Cúlo de móna, round-stern ship, an ugly shaped-craft.
Cúna, cradle.
Cuñás de mango, horsing-irons.
Cuñas de las vasádas, blocks of a ship's cradle.
Cúñas del masteléro, fids of the topmast.
Cúro, a small craft used in the south of France.
Cúrso de la maréa, tide's way.
Cúrva, knee.
Cúrva capuchína, standard of the cut-water.
Cúrva córal, knee of the stern-post.
Cúrvas á la valóna, lodging-knees.
Cúrvas verticáles de las cubiértas, hanging knees of
    the decks.
Cúrvas de los yúgos, transom-knees.
Curvedád, roach-leech, sweep.
Cúter, cutter, a small craft with one mast.

D

Dádo, palm-thimble.
Dádo de la roldána, cock of a sheave.
Dádos, corner pieces, diamond pieces
Dádos de las vélas, tablings of the bowline cringles.
Dála, pump-dale of a ship.
Damajuána, large bottle used on board ship, demijohn.
Dár culádas, the striking of a vessel against the waves.
Dár de tráste, to run aground.
Dár fuégo, to bream or fire a ship.

Dár en un bajío, to strike aground, to run aground.

Dár un raspadíllo á un bajél, to slightly scrape and clean a ship's bottom.

Dárse á la véla, to set sail.

Davánte, lateen braces.

Decaér, to fall to leeward.

Defénsas de cábo, fenders.

Dejárse caér á la pópa, to fall astern.

Dejárse caér á sotavénto, to fall to leeward.

Delgádos de un navío, the narrowing or rising of a ship's floor.

Delgádos (navío de muchos), a sharp-bottomed ship.

Demandár água, to require deeper water to sail.

Demorár, to bear in any point.

Demorár (la costa demóra al súr), the coast bears south.

Derécho, right.

Derécha la caña, right the helm.

Deríva, ship's course.

Derivár, to fall off from the course.

Derotéro, collection of sea-charts, course of a vessel.

Derribár, to cut away.

Derróta, ship's course.

Derróta estimáda, the dead reckoning of a ship.

Derrotár, to fall off.

Desabordárse, to get clear one ship from another.

Desaferrár las vélas, to unfurl the sails.

Desaforrár los cábles, to unserve the cables.

Desaguadéro, a drain.

Desaguadéros de la cebadéra, eyes of the sprit-sail.

Desahogádo, with plenty of sea-room.

Desamarrár un búque, to unmoor a vessel.

Desamarrár un cábo, to unbend a rope.

Desancorár, to weigh anchor.

Desaparejár, to strip, to unrig a ship.

Desarbolár, to unmast, to lay up a ship.

Desarbólo, the act of unmasting.

Desarbólo (sufrir un), to be dismasted at sea.

Desarrumár, to discharge a vessel.

Desartillár, to remove the guns from a man-of-war.

Desayustár, to unbend a rope.

Désca, tar-pot.

Descalabrár un navío, to disable a ship.

Descánso, boomsaddle, partner of the bowsprit.

Descansár sobre los rémos, to rest on the oars.

Descánso esteriór del bauprés, bed of the bowsprit.

Descánso interiór del bauprés, the inner partner of bowsprit.

Descánso de la caña del timón, sweep of the tiller.

Descánso (la caña tiene juégo en el), the tiller shakes.

Descárga, the discharge or the unloading of a vessel, broadside of a man-of-war.

Descargár una véla, to fill a sail.

Descolchár, to untwist.

Descosér, to unlace.

Descuarteládo (á), abaft the beam, applied to the wind.

Descubrír, to see, to make out at a distance.

Desembarcadéro, landing-place, quay.

Desembarcár, to unship, to unload.

Desembocár un estrécho, to sail out of a strait.

Desempeñárse de la tierra, to work away from the land.

Desencallár, to get a ship off that has struck on rocks.

Desentalengár, to unbend a cable.

Desenvelejár, to strip a vessel of her sails.

Desenvergár, to unbend a sail.

Desestivár, to break out the cargo stowed.

Desfalcazár, to make oakum of old ropes, to untwist.

Desfondár, to shove in, to split, to penetrate the bottom of a ship.

Desgaritár, to lose the ship's course.

Desgobernár, not to steer steadily.

Desguarnír, to unrig the capstan.

Desguindár, to slide down by a rope.

Desmantelár, to unmast.

Desmontár el timón, to unhang the rudder.

Desnudár, to unrig.

Desobedecér el timón, to fall off, not obeying the rudder.

Desobedecér (navío que desobedéce la virada), a ship that misses stays.

Despachár un búque, to get a vessel to sea.

Despachár un búque en la aduína, to clear a vessel at the custom-house.

Despasár un cábo, to unreeve a cable.

Despasár el viradór de cómbes, to shift the royal.

Despedír la génte, to pay off a ship's crew.

Despénsa, steward's room.

Despenséro, steward.

Desplegár, to unfurl.

Desplegár las vélas, to unfurl the sails.

Desplegár la bandéra, to hoist the flag.

Desrelingár, to unrope, to tare off the bolt-rope by the wind, or the violence of a storm.

Destinár un búque, to station a ship.

Destíno, station.

Destorcér, to lose the way.

Desvarár, to get a ship off that has run aground.

Desvalár, to be driven out of the course by currents.

Diagonál, cross-gore.

Díque, dock.

Díque de construcción ó díque séco, dry-dock.

Dias de pláncha, lay-days.

Días corriéntes, running days, days in succession.

Días corrídos, days of work.

Disparádo, stretched out.

Disparárse, to stretch.

Disponér las vélas al viénto, to trim the sails to the wind.

D

Disponér la bolína ciñendo al viénto, to trim the sails
    close to the wind.
Disposición, trim of a ship.
Dobléz, creasing of the seam.
Dormídos ó Durmiéntes, thick planks nailed to the
    inner ship's side, clamps.
Dormírse, to lay on her sides.
Dotación, crew, company.
Dríza, halliard or halyard.
Dríza de la mayór, main-gears.
Dríza del trinquéte, fore-gears.
Dríza de gávia, maintopsail-halliard.
Dríza del fóque, jib-halliard.
Dríza del píco, gaffpeak-halliard.
Dríza de la bóca, gaffthroat-halliard.
Dríza de bandéra, flag, or ensign-halliard.
Dríza de enténa, lateen-halliard.
Dríza del fóque mayór, throat-halliards.
Drizár, to hoist up the yards.
Dunéta, the highest part of the poop.

E

Echár á píque, to sink, to send to the bottom.
Echár en tiérra, to land anything.
Echárse sóbre áncora, to drag the anchor.
Embarcación, vessel.
Embarcación menór, boat.
Embarcár, to ship.
Embarcár un gólpe de már, to ship a sea.
Embasadúra, latchings.
Embasár, to lace on.
Embelído, eating-in, slack-cloth.

Embicár, to peek up, to top.
Embicár las vélas, to top the yards.
Embonár, to plank or sheath a ship's bottom and sides.
Embóno, planking a ship's bottom or sides, sheathing.
Embornál, scupper-hole.
Embragár, to sling.
Embravecér, to become extremely rough (the sea).
Embreár, to pay a ship with pitch.
Embrollár, to entangle.
Embrollár la bandéra, to waft the ensign.
Embutidúra, worming.
Embutír, to worm.
Empachádo (navío), an over-loaded ship.
Empalletádo, netting.
Empalomár las escárpas, to shift the scarfs.
Empalomár, to marl, to serve the bolt-rope.
Empanádo, planks laid over the well in a ship.
Empañicár, to furl.
Empavesáda, waist cloth, hammock cloth.
Empavesáda de bóte, boat's cloth.
Empavesár, to dress a ship.
Empuñadúra, ear, earing.
Empuñadúra de los rízos, reef-earing.
Empuñadúra de déntro, inner-earing.
Empuñadúra de fuéra, outer-earing.
Empuñadúra del píco, peak-earing.
Empuñadúra de la bóca, nock or neck.
Empuñadúras del gratíl, head-earings.
Enarenár, to run on the beach.
Encabezadúra, scarfing.
Encabezár, to scarf.
Encajerádo, entangled, choked (rope and pulley).
Encalladéro, shoal, sand-bank.
Encalladúra, the running on to a sandbank, and
    sticking fast.

Encallár, running on to a bank.
Encalmár, to be becalmed.
Encapilladúra, top-rigging, tie of a shroud or stay.
Encapillár, to fix the standing rigging to the masthead.
Encapillárse el água, to ship a head-sea.
Encarillár, to get entangled on shore (ropes).
Encastrár, to mortise or scarf pieces of timber.
Encerádo, tarpaulin.
Enchavetár un pérno, to forelock a bolt.
Encojér, to run up.
Encojimiénto de los costádos, the giving way of the
      sides of a ship.
Encostárse, to get near the coast.
Encrespár (la már se encréspa), to become rough (sea).
Enfangár, to stick fast in the mud.
Engalanár, to hang out all the colors.
Engalgár el áncla, to back an anchor.
Engargolár, to set rings.
Engénias, wooldings.
Engilmár, to pick up a floating mast at sea.
Engimelgár, to fish a mast, to mend a spar.
Engolfár, to get into a bay, to be surrounded by land.
Enguillár, to wind string round a rope.
Enjaretádo, grating, netting.
Enjuncár, to seize with rushes.
Enjuncár ó hacér enjúnque, to trim the hold, to ballast.
Enjúnque, ballast.
Enmalletádo, fouled (ropes).
Enmarár las vélas, to wet the sails.
Enmarárse, to get into open sea.
Enmechár, to rabbet, to fit two pieces of timber into
      one another.
Ensambladúra, a swallow-tail scarf.
⌐ ᵔsoberbecér, to become boisterous (sea).
    ᵔlingár, to fasten the cable to the anchor.

Enténa, lateen-yard.

Enterízo, single-made.

Entráda de água, a leak.

Entrañár, to worm.

Entrecubiértas, Entrepuéntes, between or 'tween decks.

Envainádo, tabled.

Envelár, to set sails.

Envergár, to bend the sails, to fasten them to the yards.

Envérgue, rope-band, robbin.

Equilibrár, to trim.

Equilíbrio, trimming.

Equipáge, crew, ship's company.

Escála, port of call.

Escála (hacér escála), to call at a port other than the port of destination.

Escála del alcazár, quarter-deck ladder.

Escála reál, accommodation-ladder.

Escála de la toldílla, poop ladder.

Escála fránca, free port.

Escalámo, thole, place to rest the oars in rowing.

Escaldrántes, kevels.

Escalimárse, working out of oakum from the seams.

Escampavía, tender.

Escandallár, to sound.

Escandállo, deep-sea lead.

Escandalósa, gaff-topsail.

Escapulár, to double a cape.

Escárba, scarf.

Escarpár, to fit timbers.

Escárpe de la quílla, scarf of the keel.

Escobén ó Escobón, hawse-hole or hawse.

Escollár, to strike a rock.

Escolléra, cliff, rocky place.

Escontréte, prop, stay.

Escoperadúras, planks nailed to the sides of a ship.

Esteperóles, scupper-nails.

Esterílla, band.

Estéro, a small creek into which the tide flows at flood-tides.

Estíma, the dead reckoning, estimation of a ship's way by the log.

Estíva, stowage, trimming, dunnage.

Estivár, to stow, to trim.

Estópa, oakum, hemp.

Estoperól, short round-headed tarpaulin nails.

Estráve, kind of wheel at the ship's head.

Estrécho, strait, a narrow arm of the sea.

Estrelléra, plain rigging without runners.

Estremíche, a piece of timber which is notched into the knees of a ship.

Estrénque, bass or sedge rope (used in America).

Estríbo, stirrup of a ship.

Estribór, starboard.

Estríbos de guardamancébos de las vérgas, stirrups of the horses.

Estríbos de los pelónes de las vérgas, stirrups of the yard-arms.

Estríbos de las cadénas, stirrups of the chain-plates, preventer-plates.

Estróvo ó Estróbo, strop or strap.

Estróvo de rémo, strap of the oars.

Estróvo de vérga, top-chain, sling of a yard.

Estróvo del pálo, snother or snotter.

Expréso, advice-boat.

F

Fácha (ponérse en), to bring to.

Fácha (en), backed.

Fácha (véla en), sail backed, or laid aback.

Facháda, front of a ship.
Facheár, to heave to, to bring to, to lie to or by.
Fája, reef-band.
Fája de rízos, reef-band.
Fája (última), close reef, low reef.
Fája de pié, foot-band, foot lining.
Fája del médio, strengthening band, middle band.
Fajeár, to band.
Falcaceár, to lash.
Fálcas, waist or wash-boards.
Falsa-amárra, preventer-rope (used to strengthen).
Falúa, barge, felucca.
Falúcho, felucco.
Faltár, to give way, to break
Faltár la viráda, to miss stays.
Fanál, lighthouse, poop-lantern.
Farallón ó Farillón, a small pointed island in the
        sea, point, cape, headland, rock, cliff.
Férro, word used sometimes instead of áncla, anchor.
Fíl de róda, right ahead.
Filáciga, rope-yarn.
Filadiér, a small boat used in France.
Filaréte, netting put on the sides of a ship.
Filástica, yarn, rope-yarn.
Fírme, main-breadth, standing.
Flameár, to drum, to shiver, to shake, to flutter.
Flaméo, shivering, shaking.
Flaúta, a Dutch three-masted craft.
Flécha, prow.
Flécha del alunamiénto, hollow, height of the foot-gore.
Flécha de la cóla de páto, height of the round.
Flechadúra, rattlings.
Flecháste, rattling or rat-line.
Fletamiénto, charter.
Fletamiénto (contráta de), charter-party.

Flór de viénto, direction of a gale of wind.

Flór (á flór de água), level with the surface of the water, at the water-edge.

Flóta, a fleet.

Flóte, afloat.

Fofóque, middle-jib.

Fogonadúra, partner of masts.

Fondeadéro, anchoring ground.

Fondeár, to cast anchor, to sound.

Fóndo, bottom, floor or flat of a ship.

Fóque, jib.

Fóque parabólico, parabolic jib.

Fóque de abaníco ó de cóncha, concentrated jib.

Fóque principál, standing-jib.

Fóque (segúndo) ó fofóque, middle-jib.

Fóque volánte, jib-o'-jib.

Fóque gránde, first jib.

Fóque segúndo, second jib.

Fóque tercéro, third jib.

Fóque de cápa, storm-jib.

Fóque de cáza, chasing-jib.

Formejár, to trim the hold.

Fórro interiór de navío, ceiling or foot-waling of a ship.

Fórro de cáble, keckling, rounding, serving.

Fórte, hold on! stop! stay!

Forzádo (corrér un viénto), to sail in a storm.

Fragáta, frigate.

Fragáta mercánte, full-rigged ship.

Franqueárse por encíma de un bájo, to get over a shoal by dint of press of sail.

Franquía, offing.

Frenillár, to bridle the oars.

Freníllo, bobstay, bridle of the oars.

Fúnda, coat, covering, hood, any case of sailcloth.

Fustága, a large rope for hoisting the mainsail.

G

Gabárra, lighter.
Galápagos, chess-trees, cleats.
Galdrópe, wheel-rope, the rope of the steering-wheel.
Galeáza, a kind of craft.
Galeótas, carlings of the hatchways.
Galéra, galley.
Galería de pópa, stern-gallery.
Galérno, soft, mild (wind).
Galíbos, models of ships, moulds.
Galíbos (sala de), mould-room.
Gallardéte, pendant, pennant, streamer.
Gallardetón, broad pendant.
Galléta, biscuit, mess-bowl.
Galón, wooden ornament on the sides of ships.
Galónes, rails around the quarter-deck.
Galópe, pole, head.
Galopín, a cabin-boy.
Gambótes, counter-timbers, arched timbers.
Gáncho, hook.
Gáncho con guardacábo, thimble-hook.
Gáncho de aparéjo, tackle-hook.
Gáncho de la gáta, cat-hook.
Gáncho giratório, swivel-hook.
Gáncho de veléro, sail-hook.
Gáncho de la botavára, goose-hook.
Gáncho de bichéro, boat-hook.
Gáncho de botalón, goose-neck of a boom.
Gáncho de las estrelléras del trinquéte, hook of the
     fore-tackle.
Gáncho de guimbaléte de las estógas, swivel-hook of
     the topsail-ties.
Gáncho de pescántes de ánclas, anchor fish-hooks.
Gánchos de las arraigádas, foot-hooks or futtocks.

Gánchos de revirár madéros, cant-hooks.
Gantéras, cheeks of the head.
Garcés, main-topsail.
Garcéta, point, reef-band, a small rope for furling sails.
Garganteadúras, throat-seizings of the blocks.
Gárra (navío de média), a vessel carrying no topsails.
Garrár, to drag, to be driven from the moorings.
Garróte de tarrajár, tap wrenches.
Garrúcho, cringle.
Garrúcho del púño de la escóta, clue-cringle.
Garrúcho del amánte de rízos, reef-tackle-cringle.
Garrúcho de la póa de bolína, bowline-cringle.
Garrúcho de madéra, hank, wooden mast-hook.
Gáta, cat, a kind of craft, cat-tackle.
Gáta (tíro del aparéjo de la), cat-fall.
Gáta (cuadernál de la), cat-block.
Gáta (enganchár la gáta en el áncla), to cat the anchor.
Gáto, jack-screw.
Gávia, main-topsail.
Gávia volánte, save-all-topsail.
Gaviéro, top-man.
Gaviéro mayór de la cófa del trinquéte, captain of
    the fore-top.
Gaviéta, scuttle.
Gaviéte del bauprés, saddle of the bowsprit.
Gavilánes, tholes.
Gavióta, a sea-gull.
Gáza, eye-splice, loop, strap.
Gáza de motón, stay of a block.
Gáza de estái, collar of a stay.
Gemélos, cheeks or side-beams of the masts.
Generála, signal to join a convoy.
Genóles, futtocks.
Gimélga, fish, rubbing-paunch, pieces of timber to
    strengthen masts and spars.

Gobernár, to steer.
Goléta, a fore-and-aft schooner.
Goléta de gávias, a main-topsail schooner.
Goléta de velácho, a topsail schooner.
Golílla, partner's-rim.
Gráda de constrúccion, stocks for shipbuilding.
Gráda (navío en la), ship on the stocks.
Grangeár, to gain to windward.
Gratíl, head, stay, luff of a sail.
Gratíl de vérga, hound.
Gregalizár, to decline or drive to the north-east.
Gribár, to fall to leeward.
Grímpola, vane, a sort of weathercock.
Grípo, a kind of craft now rarely in use.
Groéra, hole.
Grúa, bend of a piece of timber of peculiar shape.
Grúa de la cuadérna maéstra, midship-bend.
Gruéras, rope-holes.
Gruéras de barbiquéjo, bobstay-holes.
Gruméte, ship's boy.
Guaíra, sliding-gunter sail, shoulder-of-mutton sail.
Guaíro, name of a small craft on the coast of Cuba.
Gualdéras de las carlingas, sides of the carlings.
Gualdrapázo, jerk, slap of the sails against the masts.
Gualdrapeár, to slap against the masts (sails).
Guardacábo, thimble.
Guardacóstas, revenue vessel.
Guardahúmo, smoke sail.
Guardamancébo, man-rope, horse, entering-rope.
Guárdabauprés, knightheads, bollard-timbers.
Guardacadénas, chain-stoppers.
Guardainfántes, capstan whelps.
Guardajárcia, racks of the shrouds.
Guardamancébos de sondeár, breastropes for sounding.
Guardamancébos de las vérgas, foot-ropes or horses.

Guardatimónes, stern-chains.
Guardavéla, a small rope for furling the topsails.
Guardia marína, midshipman.
Guardián del contramaéstre, boatswain's mate.
Guardín de la caña, tiller-rope.
Guardínes, wheel-ropes, tiller-ropes.
Guárne, running part.
Guarnés, turns of a tackle-fall.
Guarnimiénto, rigging, serving.
Guarnír, to rig a sail or tackle.
Guarnír el cabrestánte, to rig the capstan.
Gubiadúra del tamboréte, channel of a cap.
Gubiadúra de un motón, notch of a block.
Guía, guy, hauling-line, a small rope.
Guía de falsa amárra, guest-rope.
Guimbaléte, handle of a pump.
Guínda, hoist, taunt.
Guindádo, hoisted.
Guindádo (los masteléros están guindádos), the top-
        masts are set up.
Guindaléza, hawser-laid rope.
Guindár, to send up, to topsail, to hoist, to raise aloft.
Guiñáda, yawing, deviation from the right course.
Guiñár, to yaw.
Guión, loom of an oar.
Gurrár, to get clear of another ship.

H

Hacér água, to leak.
Hachuéla, boarding-axe.
Halár, to haul.
Halár el bóte á bórdo, to haul the boat on board.
Halár al viénto, to haul the wind.

Harpéo, grapnel, grappling-iron.
Hamáca, cot.
Henchimiéntos, timbers used to fill the hollow parts
    of a ship's frame, filling timbers.
Herír el cásco de un navío, to hull a ship.
Herráge de un navío, ironwork of a ship.
Hílo de una corriénte, the main course of a current.
Hójas de las puértas, port-lids.
Hónda, a sling used for shipping goods.
Horquéta, crotche, saddleboom, outrigger.
Horquíllas, crotches.
Horquíllas del fóndo, fore-crotches.
Hucár, hooker, a kind of Dutch craft.
Husíllo, snock, spencer-mast, trysailmast.

I

Imádas, sliding-planks used in launching ships.
Imbornáles, scupper-holes, scuppers.
Imbornál de bómba, pump scupper-hole.
Imbornáles de varéngas, limber-holes.
Imperiál, poop-royal.
Imperiál, name given to all Austrian vessels in the
    Mediterranean.
Insígnia, distinguishing-flag.
Izár, to hoist, to heave, to draw up.

J

Jabéga, small xebeck.
Jabéque, xebeck, a small three-masted vessel in the
    Mediterranean.
Járcia, cordage, rope rigging, tackle.
Járcia muérta ó de fírme, standing ropes or rigging.

Járcia de labór, running rigging.
Járcia mayór, main-rigging.
Járcias de respéto, spare-rigging.
Járcias (táblas de), set of rigging.
Jardín, quarter-gallery.
Jardínes de pópa, quarter-galleries.
Jaréta, catharping or catharpins, netting.
Jarétas del pié de las arraigádas, catharpings.
Jórro (ír á), to be towed.
Juanéte, topgallantsail.
Juanéte mayór, main-topgallantsail.
Juanéte de próa, fore-topgallantsail.
Juanéte de sobremesána, mizen-topgallantsail.
Juanéte vólánte, flying-topgallantsail.
Jubertár, to hoist the boat on board.
Juégo de vélas, set of sails.
Jumelár, to strengthen masts with partners.
Jumélos, partners.
Juntúra, scarf.

L

Laboreár, to run, to work a ship.
Laboréo, the running, the working of a ship.
Lampaceár, to swab, to clean the deck.
Lampázo, swab, mop.
Láncha, launch, longboat, barge, lighter.
Láncha de socórro, life-boat.
Lanchón, lighter or barge.
Lanción, a kind of guard-ship in India.
Lanílla, bunting.
Lantéon, jigger-tackle, furling-line.
Lanzamiénto, rake of stem, length of a ship.
Largár, to let go, to loosen, to let out, to slacken.

Largár en bánda, to let go quickly.
Largár una véla, to loose, to unfurl a sail.
Largár véla, to set sail.
Largár los rízos, to shake out the reefs.
Largár las brázas de la gávia, to let go the main-topsail braces.
Largár (tóda véla lárga), all sails out.
Lárgo, length.
Lárgo (á un), quarter, large.
Lascár, to draw down, to ease off, to slacken.
Lascár el viradór de cómbes, to surge the capstan.
Lascón, check, surge.
Lástra, boat, lighter.
Lastrár, to ballast.
Lastrár (véla de), port-sail.
Lastrár (láncha de), ballast lighter.
Lástre, ballast.
Latína, lateen-sail.
Latíno, a craft with lateen-sails.
Latitúd, latitude.
Latitúd por encíma, latitude by dead reckoning.
Latitúd arribáda, latitude reached.
Latónes, laths, ledges used on board ship.
Laúd, small lateen boat.
Lesuéste, east-south-east wind.
Léva, the weighing of the anchor, swell of the sea.
Levár él áncla, to weigh the anchor.
Liébre, racks or ribs, dead-eyes.
Liénza, sham line, marking line.
Liénzo, sailcloth.
Liénzo de Rusía, duck, Russian duck.
Ligadúra, the lashing, the seizing.
Liméra, helm port, rudder hole.
Limonáge, boats piloting a ship into port.
Linéa de água, water or level line.

Linéa de cárga, load-water line.
Linéa de la astílla muérta, the cutting-down line.
Linéa de los revéses del costáda, the top-timber lines.
Linguéte, paul ó parol; a short bar of wood or iron
   put into the capstan to prevent it rolling back.
Lísta del equipáge, muster-book of a ship.
Listónes, battens.
Listónes de las escotíllas, battens of the hatchways.
Llamár (el viénto lláma á pópa), the wind veers aft.
Llamár (el viénto lláma á próa), the wind hauls forward.
Lláve, knee.
Lláves, cross-stitches.
Llevár, to carry.
Llevár la próa al súr, to stand to the south.
Llevár las vélas á buén viénto, to fill the sails.
Llevár las vélas llénas, to keep the sails full.
Lóf ó Ló, the weather-side of a ship, loof.
Lóf (amúra del), weather-tack.
Lóf (no más de), not nearer to the wind.
Lómo, edge.
Lóna, canvas, sailcloth.
Lóna de refuérzo, lining canvas.
Lonéta, raven's duck.
Lúa, leeside.
Lúa (tomár por la), chapelling, to bring to the lee.
Luchadéro, ó Luidéro, friction-place.
Luchíllo, goring, goring-cloth.
Lúgre, lugger.
Luír, to chafe, to gall, to wear by friction.
Lumbréra, skylight.

M

Macarrónes, awning-stanchions.
Macéta, maul, mallet.

Macéta de aferrár, serving mallet.
Macéta de calafáte, a caulking-mallet.
Macéta de ayustár, a driving-mallet.
Mácho del timón, rudder-pintles.
Madéra de construcción, timber for shipbuilding.
Madéra de respéto, spare masts.
Mádre del timón, main-piece of the rudder.
Mádre de vuélta del timón, barrel of the steering-wheel.
Maéstro veléro, sailmaker.
Maestralizár, to vary to west or north-west (compass).
Maéstre ó patrón, ship-master, captain of merchantman.
Maéstre de raciónes, purser.
Magújo, rave-hook; to pick out the old oakum.
Málla, network of a ship.
Mambrú, part of the galley chimney that reaches
    over the deck.
Mámparo, bulkhead.
Mámparo de pópa al mámparo de próa (del), from
    stem to stern.
Mancár, to miss, to fail.
Mandarria, iron maul, a heavy iron hammer.
Mandríles, mastertaps.
Mánga de un búque, main breadth of a ship.
Manguéra, windsail, ventilator, canvas hose, pump
    hose.
Manifiésto de un búque, ship's manifest, an enumera-
    tion and specification of the entire cargo; a
    copy of the bills of lading of the ship's cargo.
Maniguétas, kevels on the quarter-deck.
Manila, lateen sail flamish-eye.
Manióbra, rigging.
Manióbra fírme, standing rigging.
Manióbra volánte, running rigging.
Manióbra (un búque que manióbra bién), a ship
    that works well.

Maniobrár, to work, to manœuvre a ship.

Manióbras altas, upper running rigging.

Manióbras bájas, lower-running rigging.

Manióbras de caréna, careening-gear

Manióbras de combáte, preventer-rigging.

Maniobrísta, a naval tactician.

Maniquetónes, snatch-cleats.

Máno (de la buéna), right-handed.

Máno (de la mála), left-handed.

Máno sobre máno, hand-over-hand.

Manúbrio, crank.

Maragúto, jib.

Márcha de un búque, the headway of a ship, the distance run in a day.

Márcha (el búque tiéne buéna), the ship sails well.

Marchapié, horse, foot-rope.

Maréa, tide.

Maréa creciénte, flood-tide.

Maréa menguánte, ebb-tide.

Maréa paráda, slack-tide.

Maréa (canál de), tide-way or tide channel.

Mareár, to trim, to fill the sails.

Marejáda, a great swell in the sea, a heavy head-sea.

Margaríta, messenger (a rope).

Maricangálla, ring-tailsail.

Marína, marine, navy.

Marinéro, seaman, sailor, tar.

Maríno, maritime, belonging to the sea, seafaring man.

Martíllo, bunt, depth of the luff.

Mascárse, to chafe.

Masteléro, mast.

Masteléro mayór ó de gávia, main-topmast.

Masteléro de juanéte, top-gallantmast.

Masteléro de velácho, fore-topmast.

Masteléro de sobremesána, mizen-topmast.

Masteléro de juanéte mayór, main-topgallantmast.
Masteléro de juanéte de próa, fore-topgallantmast.
Masteléro de juanéte de sobremesána, mizen-top-
    gallantmast.
Masteléro de sobrejuanéte mayór, main-royalmast.
Masteléro de sobrejuanéte de próa, fore-royalmast.
Masteléro de sobreperiquíto, mizen-royalmast.
Masteléro enterízo, single mast.
Masteléro de respéto, spare topmast.
Matafión, gasket.
Matafión de tóldo, awning gasket.
Matasoldádos, mizen-staysail.
Matrícula, register, matriculation.
Mayór, mainsail.
Mayór redóndo, main course
Mayór cangréja, mainsail.
Mayór de cápa, storm-mainsail.
Mayóres, courses.
Mázo, heaving-mallet.
Mécha, tenon.
Médio (á médio náo), midships.
Ména, girt or size of cordage.
Menguánte, ebb-tide.
Mensagéro, bull's-eye, traveller, a wooden thimble.
Meollár, yarn, spun yarn.
Mérlin, marling-line or marline.
Mésa, hound.
Mésa de guarnicíon, channel bend, chain-wale.
Mesána, mizzen or mizen, driver, spanker.
Mesána de cápa, mizen-trysail, storm-driver.
Mesána redónda, cross-jacksail.
Mésas de guarnición del pálo mayór, main chain-wales.
Mésas de guarnición del trínquéte, fore chain-wales.
Mílla, mile or knot.
Mística, settee.

Móco, dolphin-striker, martíngale.
Mogóte, a solitary flat-browed rock at sea.
Molinéte, windlass.
Montár un cábo, to double a cape.
Montár un navío, to take command of a ship.
Montéra, skysail.
Mordáza, rubber.
Mordér, to bite, to hold fast.
Mortéro, pump-box.
Mortéro de brújula, inner compass-box.
Mostáchos, standing-lifts.
Mostáchos del bauprés, bowsprit shrouds.
Motón, block, single block.
Motón de palóma, tie-block.
Motón de rabíza, tail-block.
Motón ciégo, dead-block.
Motón de gáncho, hook-block.
Motón de aparéjo, tackle-block.
Motón de amantíllo, lift-block.
Motón de la gáta, cat-block.
Motón del viradór del tamboréte, top-block.
Motónes herrádos, iron-bound blocks.
Motónes de retómbo, leading-blocks.
Motónes de aparéjo de cómbes, winding-tackle blocks.
Motónes de cáñas de la cebadéra, spritsail sheet-blocks.
Motónes de la dríza mayór, main-gear-block.
Motónes de los palanquínes de las vélas mayóres,
    clue-garnet blocks.
Motonería, set or assortment of blocks.
Mózo, a boy ; also used for an able seaman.
Muélle, pier, quay, mole, key, wharf.
Muérto, the groundways.
Muérto (óbra muérta), the bulwarks.
Muléta, mullet, winch used to spin yarn.
Múra, tack, bow, luff.

N

Náve, ship.
Navegár, to sail, to navigate.
Navegár arribádo, to bear away large.
Navegár arrizádo, to be close-reefed.
Navegár con viénto de través, to sail by the wind, or on the wind, abreast the wind.
Navegár en pópa, to sail free, or before the wind, both sheets aft.
Navegár a un lárgo, to sail large, to sail free.
Navegár a bolína agarrocháda, to be on a taut bowline, to sail close-hauled.
Naviéro, proprietor of a ship.
Navío, ship of war, man-of-war, ship of the line.
Navío de tres puéntes, three-decked ship.
Navío de álto bórdo, line-of-battle ship.
Navío de almacén, store-ship.
Navío de traspórte, transport.
Navío guardacósta, guard-ship
Navió de carga, ship of burthen.
Navío pesádo, a bad sailer.
Nérvio, a small rope fixed to a stay.
Nérvio de una vérga, jack-stay.
Nérvio del tóldo, awning-side ropes.
Nérvio de véla latína, strengthening-line.
Norteár, to steer to the northward.
Noruesteár, to decline to the north-west (the needle).
Núdo, hitch, bend, knot, mile.

O

Obénques, shrouds.
Obencadúra, a complete set of shrouds.

Obra muérta, dead-work, upperwork, free-board.
Obra víva, quick-work.
Obradór de vélas, sail loft.
Obradór, workshop.
Obras de maréa, grid-iron work.
Oéste, the west.
Oéste cuárta al nórte, west by nórth.
Oéste cuárta al súr, west by south.
Oéste sudéste, west-south-west.
Ojéte, hole.
Ojo, eye-splice, earing-splice.
Ojo de gáza, eye of a strap.
Ojo de la cúña del masteléro, the fid hole of a mast.
Olláo, eyelet-hole.
Olláos de los rízos, reef-eyelet holes.
Oréjas del áncla, flukes of the anchor.
Orientár, to trim a sail, to set a sail.
Orientár una véla, to trim a sail.
Orientár (navío bién orientádo á la bolína), a sharp-
    trimmed ship.
Orientación, trimming.
Oriénte, the east.
Orígen del viénto, the wind's eye.
Orílla, selvage, edge of a sail.
Orínque, buoy-rope.
Ortodromía, orthodromy, sailing in a straight course.
Orzáda, the coming to, or up.
Orzadéras, lee-boards.
Orzapópa, lateen-brace.
Orzár, to luff, to come to the wind, to bear away.
Orzár á la bánda, hard a-lee.
Orzár tódo, to keep the luff, to keep the wind.
Ostaga, tie, runner.
Ostas, lateen-braces, vangs.

P

Pabellón, national flag or colors.
Pacotílla, a small parcel of goods shipped on spec.
Páge, cabin-boy.
Pailebót, pilot's boat, bermudoe-rigged boat.
Pairár ó Capeár, to lay to.
Paíro (al), the act of lying to.
Pajarél, rope fastened to the corner of a sail.
Pajes, broad-seams.
Palanquín, clue-garnet.
Palánca, strong rope at the stays of a sail.
Palazón, the masting or masts of ships in general.
Paléta de azotár, cobbing-board (to punish sailors).
Paléta de ferrár, serving board.
Palléta, mat, paunch.
Palmajáres de los escárpes, scarf-thickstuff.
Palmajáres de los durmiéntos, clamp-thickstuff.
Palmeár, to measure down.
Palmejár, thick-stuff, a thick plank nailed along the
  inner sides of a vessel.
Palmejáres del plan, floor-thickstuff.
Pálo, mast.
Pálo mayór, mainmast.
Pálo trinquéte, foremast.
Pálo mesána, mizenmast.
Pálo bauprés, bowsprit.
Pálo mácho, polemast, blockmast.
Pálo típle ó enterízo, polemast.
Pálo de piézas, mademast.
Pálo (á pálo séco) to run before the wind without
  sails, or under bare poles.
Pálo reforzádo, fished mast.
Pálo en bruto, rough mast.

Pálos principáles, the lower or standing masts.

Palóma, sling of a yard.

Palomadúras, seams of the sails, where the boltrope is sewed to them.

Pánas imbornaléras de las varéngas, limber-boards.

Pánas de bóte, boat timber-boards.

Pánda, slack.

Pandéo, slack, bulge.

Páño, cloth, canvas, sail-cloth.

Páño de brúsca, cloth-gored, goring-cloth.

Páño cuadrádo, square cloth.

Páño de cuchíllo, leech cloth.

Páño del gratíl, head cloth.

Páño del pujámen, foot cloth.

Paño (el bárco va con poco paño), the vessel carries little sail.

Páñol, room in a vessel for keeping stores.

Páñol de vélas, sail-room.

Pañol de pólvora, powder magazine.

Pañol de próa, boatswain's store-room.

Pañol del condestable, gunner's room.

Pantóque, floor of the vessel.

Pápo de viénto, a small sail.

Parapéto, netting or parapet.

Parchaménto, trim of the ship when the sails are backed.

Partída, crew of a ship, gang.

Partír las amárras, to part the cable.

Pasadéra, lacing-line.

Pasadór, fid, splicing-fid, marling-spike, marling-fid.

Paságe, passage, passage-money.

Pasamáno, gangway.

Pasár un cábo, to reeve a rope, to pass it through a block.

Pasavolánte, fagot, a seaman entered in the muster-book but fictitious, false muster.

Pastéca, snatch-block.

Páta de gánso, claw.

Patáche, coaster, tender.

Patarraéz, preventer-shroud.

Patarraéz de una maquína de arbolár, the shroud of a sheer-hulk for masting ships.

Patésca, a large block.

Patílla, spike nailed to the sternpost on which the helm moves.

Patrón, master.

Patrón de bóte, cockswain.

Pavesádas, waistclothes for shelter.

Pavesádas de las cósas, top-armour of the lower masts.

Peána de las muniquétas, step of the kevels.

Péna, lee-arm, after-end, peak.

Péna de la mesána, peak of the mizen.

Péndola (dár péndolas á un navío), to boot-top a ship.

Pendón reál, parliament-heel, boot-topping.

Pendúra, slack.

Penól, yard-arm.

Pérchas, floor-timbers.

Perdér (la maréa piérde) the tide falls.

Perdérse, to be shipwrecked.

Perigállo, triving-line, navel-line, topping-lift.

Perílla, acorn.

Periquíto, mizen-topgallantsail, staysail.

Periquíto de juanéte mayór, flying-staysail.

Periquíto de sobremesána, mizen-topgallant-staysail.

Períto, a surveyor, an inspector, a practical experienced man who is named umpire in case of dispute.

Perlongár, to sail along the coast.

Pernéte, small pin, peg or bolt.

Pérno, bolt.

Pérno de roldána, pin of a block, sheave axle-tree.

Pérno de gáncho, hook-bolt.

Pérno de ójo, eye-bolt.

Pérno de argólla, ring-bolt.

Pérno de cadéna, chain-bolt.

Perroquéte, top-mast.

Pescánte, davit, a piece of timber used to haul up the flukes of an anchor.

Pescánte de la amúra, bumkin or boomkin.

Péso muérto, dead weight, part of a ship's cargo weighing many times more than it measures.

Péso (toneládas de péso y medída), tons weight and measurement.

Pespuntár, to back-stitch.

Pespúnte, back-stitch.

Petifóque, flying-jib.

Picár los pálos, to cut away the masts.

Píchola, storm-lateensail.

Píco, gaff.

Píco del áncla, bill of the anchor.

Picóta, cheek of pump.

Pié de carnéro, samson's post.

Pié derécho, stanchion.

Pié de róda, fore-foot, end of the fore-part of the keel.

Piézas de respéto, spare gear.

Pilóto, mate, pilot.

Pináza, pinnace.

Píngüe, pink, a vessel with a very narrow stern.

Pínola de cabrestánte, capstan-spindle.

Pínola de cuádrante, vane of a quadrant.

Píña, wall-knot, a peculiar knot at the end of a rope.

Pióla, house-line, housing.

Pipería, casks, gang casks.

Pique (írse á), to sink, to founder, to go to the bottom.

Píque (echár á), to sink a vessel.

Píques, crotches.

Pirágua, a kind of small craft.

Placél, sandbank or rocks in the sea.

Plán de las varéngas, flat of floor-timbers.

Plán (un búque de múcho), a very flat-floored ship.

Plána (navegación), plane navigation.

Pláncha, stage, a set of boards for taking in cargo, serving as a kind of bridge from the wharf.

Pláncha de água, punt, floating-stage.

Pláncha de desembarcár, gang-board.

Pláncha de viénto, hanging-stage.

Pláncha (días de), lay days.

Plancháda, framing or apron of a gun.

Planchár, to rub down.

Plánes, flat floor-timbers.

Pláno de velámen, plan of sail.

Plantílla, mould, pattern for the curve of a ship's frame.

Planúdo, a very flat-bottomed vessel.

Pleamár ó Plenamár, high-water.

Plúma, relieving-tackle.

Póas, bridles of the bowlines.

Polácra, polacre, a three-masted craft used in the Mediterranean.

Poléa, pulley.

Polín, a wooden roller for moving heavy things.

Poniénte, the west, the west wind.

Pontón, a floating depôt, a flat-bottomed boat with appliances for cleaning harbours, etc.

Pópa, stern.

Pópa llána, flat quarter, square-sterned.

Pópa redónda, round quarter.

Pópa (á), aft, abaft.

Pópa (hácia, por la), aft, abaft, astern.

Pópa (de próa á), fore-and-aft, from stem to stern.

Pópa (pasár por la) to pass under a ship's stern.

Pópa (quedárse por la), to drop astern.

Pópa (vélas de), after-sails.

Pópa (viénto en), wind aft, before the wind.

Popél, aft.

Popéses, stays of the mizenmast.

Portár, to carry, to fill.

Pórtas del acastillágo, gun-ports of the quarter-deck and forecastle.

Pórtas de las míras de próa, head chase-ports.

Pórtas de lastrár, ballast-ports.

Pórtas de embarcár madéra, raft-ports, timber ports.

Pórtas de guardatimón, stern-ports.

Pórtas, gun-ports.

Portálo ó Portatón, gangway.

Portañóla, port-hole.

Portañólas de los camarótes, light-ports.

Portañólas de los rémos, row-ports.

Portár bién, to carry well, to be a good sea boat.

Pórte de quiniéntas toneládas, 500 tons burthen.

Pórte de dos míl cájas de azúcar, carries 2000 boxes of sugar.

Pórte, rate, tonnage, burthen.

Posteléro, skids.

Posteléros de las amúras, chess-trees.

Pózo (navío de), a deep-waisted ship.

Pózo de cáble, cable-stage, cable-tier.

Práctico, pilot.

Precínta, parcelling.

Precintár, to parcel.

Presupuésto, estimate, memorial.

Próa, head, prow.

Próa (á), fore, afore.

Próa (hácia, por la), forward, ahead, afore.

Próa (por la cára de), forward, fore-part.

Próa (de pópa á), fore-and-aft, from stem to stern.

Proél, fore or headmost part of a ship, seaman stationed at the prow.

Proís, breast-fast (a rope).
Proíza, cable at the head of a slip fastened to the anchor.
Propáo, breast-work.
Próra, head, prow.
Puénte, deck of a ship.
Puénte á la oréja, flush-deck.
Puénte de enjaretáda, grating-deck.
Puénte de rédes, netting-deck.
Pujámen, foot, under part of the sails.
Puntáda, stitch.
Puntál, depth of hold, stanchion.
Punteár, to catch the wind.
Púnto, stitch.
Púnta de vaína, long-work.
Púnto de telár, close-work, small long-work.
Púnto de bigorrílla, round stitch.
Púnto de espáda, point in zigzag.
Púntos cruzádos, cross-stitch.
Punzón, pegging-awl, pricker, punch.
Púño, clue or clew, each of the lower points of a
     sail in which the tacks are fastened.
Púño de la amúra, tack.
Púño de la bóca, nock or neck.
Púño de la escóta, clue.
Púño del gratíl, earing.
Púño del píco, peak or peek.
Púño de la pína, head.
Púño de garrúcho, clue-cringle.
Púño de gáza, turned clue.
Púño (partir al), to fly up to the wind, to gripe.
Púños altos, earings.
Púños bájos, clues.
Púños de las pájas, reef cringles.

Q

Quebránte, cambering of a ship's deck or keel.
Quéche, ketch or quaiche, a kind of Dutch craft.
Quechemarín, coasting vessel with three masts on the coast of Spain.
Quechemarína, storm mainsail.
Quijádas, taws, horns.
Quílla, keel.
Quináles, preventer-shrouds.

R

Rabizá, the point or end of a rope.
Rabíza (motón de), tail-block.
Rabíza de bandéra, tack of a flag, downhaul.
Rábo de gállo, broad pendant, stern-timbers.
Rábo de ráta, pointed rope.
Ráca, traveller.
Ráca de la amúra, jib-iron.
Racaménto, parral or parrel.
Racaménto (bastárdo de), parrel rope. •
Racéles, run of a ship.
Radéro, a ship that rides well at anchor.
Ráfa de viénto, a gust of wind.
Ráfaga, a squall, a sudden gust.
Ráncho, mess-room.
Ráncho de santa bárbara, gun-room.
Ránda, mainsail in a schooner (Italian word).
Ranúra, notch, score, channel.
Rascanúbes ó Rascaciélos, sky-scrapers.
Rascatréra, lower-studdingsail, save all, water sail.

Rasél, narrow part of a ship towards the head and stern.

Rasquéta, scraper.

Rástra, creeper, a sort of grappling-iron with which a lost anchor is fished up.

Rastrár, to drag for an anchor.

Ratón, a hidden rock.

Reátas, woolding, ropes fastened round a mast to give it strength.

Rebasadéro, a dangerous place to pass.

Rebénque, fox, rope with which seamen are flogged.

Rebénque de pórtas, port-rope.

Rebéza, alteration in the currents on a coast.

Rebózo de calafáte, drive-bolt (used by caulkers).

Recaláda, landfall, making the land.

Recalár, to stand in-shore.

Reclamár, to hoist home, to hoist atrip.

Recláme, sheave-hole in a topmast-head.

Reclámo, tie-block.

Recobrár, to rouse in, to take up a loose end of a rope.

Recorrér un búque, to repair a ship.

Recorrér los cábles, to under-run the cables.

Recorrér (buque en recorrída) a ship under repairs.

Reculár, to stern away, to go aback, to make sternway.

Réd, net or netting.

Redél, loof-frame.

Redónda, square-sail.

Reflújo, ebb, reflux, backward course of water.

Reflújo (flújo y reflújo), full and low tide.

Refórzar, to strengthen.

Refrescár, to freshen.

Refrescár los cábles, to freshen the hawse.

Refrésco, fresh provisions.

Refuérzos, linings.

Refuérzos de los brióles, buntline-cloths.

Refuérzos de los amántes de rízos, reef-tackle pieces.

F

Regála, gunwale or gunnel.

Regateár, to compare the sailing powers of two crafts, to rival in sailing.

Regéra, stern-fast, stern-moorings.

Regír ó Gobernár, to obey the helm.

Relínga, bolt-rope.

Relínga del gratíl, head-line, head-bolt-rope.

Relínga del pujámen, foot-bolt-rope.

Relínga de las caídas, leech-bolt-rope.

Relingár, to rope a sail.

Relónga del pujámen, foot-rope.

Relónga de caída, leech-rope.

Relónga de la valúma, leech-rope.

Relónga del pálo, mast-rope.

Relónga de la caída de próa, foreleech-rope.

Relónga de la caída de pópa, afterleech-rope.

Relónga del púño, clue-rope.

Relónga de cúmbre, ridge-rope.

Relónga de bandéra, tack of a flag.

Remendár, to mend the sails, to line.

Remiéndo, lining.

Rémo, oar.

Rémo (pála de un), wash of an oar.

Rémo (manuál de un), handle of an oar.

Remolcár, to tow.

Remolcadór (vapór remolcadór), tug-boat.

Remolínos del timón, wake.

Rempújo, palm.

Rendír, to spring a mast.

Repuntár, to begin to ebb.

Repuésto (mádera de), spare timber.

Resáca, surge, surf.

Resón, a small anchor for boats.

Respéto (masteléro de), spare topmast.

Respéto (pertréchos de), spare stores.

Retenída, guy.
Retenída de próa, head-fast.
Revés del tajamár, hollow of the cut-water.
Revéses de la estéla, eddy of the dead-water.
Rezón, grappling, fastening.
Rifadúra, the furling of a sail, the splitting of a sail.
Rifárse, to split.
Rízos, points.
Rízos (tomár), to reef.
Rízos (largár), to shake the reefs.
Rízos chicos, close-reef, low-reef, bag-reef.
Róda ó Róa, stem.
Rodíllas, knees of ship timber.
Roldána, sheave.
Ronceár, to sail badly.
Roncería, sluggish sailing.
Rónza, the state of a vessel at the mercy of the
        wind and tide.
Ronzál, a strong rope at the stays of a sail.
Ronzár, to haul in without the aid of tackle.
Roña, garland.
Roñáda de ráncho, mess-garland.
Roñáda de la guirnálda de un pálo, dolphin of a mast.
Rósa nautíca, card of a mariner's compass.
Rósca de cáble, flake of a cable.
Rósca de már, sea-rusk, biscuit.
Roséga, creeper, a kind of grapnel.
Róta, course.
Rozadúra, chafing.
Rozádo, chafed, fretted, galled.
Rozár, to chafe, to gall, to rag (cables).
Ruéca (armár una), to fish a mast or yard.
Ruéda, steering-wheel.
Rúmbo, rhumb-line, course, point of the compass.

S

Sacabúche, tube used as a pump.
Sacanábo, pump-hook.
Sáco, belly, bag part of a sail, drop of a sail.
Saetía, saick, settee, vessel used in the Mediterranean.
Salída, headway, rapidity.
Salóma, the singing-out of sailors.
Salomár, to sing out.
Salomónicos, puckering.
Saltár, to check, to surge.
Saltár (el viénto sálta), the wind changes from one
        quarter to another, suddenly.
Saltár (sálte génte á la bánda), man the ship's sides.
Sálto, check, surge.
Sálto de viénto, the sudden shifting of the wind.
Sálto (dár un sálto á la bolína), to check the bowline.
Salvachía, sling, salvage.
Sánta bárbara, powder-magazine on board a ship.
Santélmo (fuégo de), an electric light that appears
        sometimes at the yard and mast-ends.
Sardinéla, lanyard.
Sarangósti, a kind of gum used in lieu of pitch.
Sardinéta, knittle, a small line.
Sébo, tallow.
Séco (corrér á pálo séco), to scud under bare poles.
Séno, bight, slack, curvature of a sail.
Sentína, the well where the pump-pipes draw.
Señalár, to crease, to plait, to signal.
Señáles de brúma, fog signals.
Serrétas, pieces of tarred canvas.
Servióla, cathead, watchman.
Singladúra, a watch, a day's run.

Singlár, to progress steadily with a fair wind in a direct course.

Síngle, single.

Singlón, timber placed over the keel.

Sírga, tow-rope, tow-line.

Sírga (á la), sailing with a dragging line.

Sirgadúra, the towing or hauling of a barge along the banks of a river or canal.

Sirgár, to tow or drag a ship along by means of a rope.

Sobrancéro, slack.

Sobrecárgo, supercargo.

Sobrecebadéra, sprit-topsail.

Sobrecosér, to flatten.

Sobreescandalósa, gaff-topgallantsail.

Sobreestadías, days of demurrage.

Sobrejuanétes, royals.

Sobremesána, mizen-topsail.

Sóbremuñonéra, clamp or cap-square of a cannon.

Sobreperiquíto, mizen-royal.

Sobreplán, rider.

Sobrequílla, keelson or kelson.

Sobresános, leech-linings, broad hem on sails.

Sóbres, royals.

Sobretrancaníles, spirketing or spirket-rising.

Sobreventár, to gain the weather-guage of another ship.

Sobreviénto, weather-guage.

Socaíre, slatch, loose part of a rope.

Socár, to set a rope taut.

Socolláda, jerk, violent straining of ropes.

Soldáda, the wages of sailors.

Solér, underflooring of a ship.

Soléra, foot-rails of the gallery of a ship.

Solládo de los pañóles de la despénsa, cockpit.

Solládo, orlop.

Soltár (el áncla ha soltádo el fóndo), the anchor is a-weigh.

Sombréro, top, hat-money, prímage.
Sónda, sounding.
Sónda del escandállo, lead soundings.
Sónda (navegár en sónda por la sondalésa), to sail
    by the log.
Sondalésa, lead-line.
Sondalésa de máno, hand-lead.
Sondalésa de la bómba, guage-rod of the pump.
Sondár ó Sondeár, to sound, to throw the lead.
Sóplos, catspaws.
Sórra, ballast of stones or coarse gravel.
Sotacómitre, boatswain's mate.
Sotaventádo, driven to leeward.
Sotaventár, to fall to leeward.
Sotavénto, lee.
Sotavénto (á), to leeward, under the lee.
Sotavénto (tenér buén), to have plenty of sea-room.
Sotavénto (bánda de), lee-side.
Sotavénto (cósta de), lee-shore.
Subfletár, to sub-charter.
Súd, south.
Sudoéste, south-west.
Sudoéste cuárto al oéste, south-west by west.
Sudoéste cuárto al súr, south-west by south.
Suéste, south-east.
Suéste cuárto al éste, south-east by east.
Suéste cuárto al súr, south-east by south.
Sumáca, smack.
Súncho, hoop, iron band.
Súncho de las arraigádos, chain-necklaces, futtock
    shroud hoop
Súnchos de la bómba, pump-clamps.
Súnchos de los botalónes de las álas, studdingsail-
    boom irons.
Súnchos de cabrestánte, capstan-hoops.

Súnchos del cépo del áncla, anchor-stock hoops.
Súnchos de fogonadúras, partners.
Súnchos de los pálos, mast-hoops.
Súr, south.
Surgír, to anchor.
Súrto, lying at anchor, anchored.

T

Tabládo, platform.
Tabládo de la cirugía, cockpit.
Tablazón de la cubiérta, deck-plank.
Tablazón esteriór, outside-planking.
Tablazón de los fóndos, floor-planking.
Tablazón interiór ó fórro, inside-planking, ceiling.
Tácos de los escobénes, hawse-plugs.
Tafúrea, a kind of flat-bottomed boat.
Tajamár, knee of the head, cut-water.
Tajamár (escóras del), props of the cut-water.
Talón (dár con el talón en el fóndo), to touch ground
       with the sternpost.
Tálla, large block.
Tallaviénto, stormsail of a lugger.
Tamboréte, cap of the masthead.
Tangidéra, cable.
Tangón, lower-studdingsail-boom.
Taquétes, cleats.
Tarquína, lugsail.
Tartána, tartan, coasting vessel in the Mediterranean.
Teléra de aráña, dead-eye of a crowfoot.
Tempestád, a violent wind, tempest.
Templadéra, sluice in a canal to let out water.
Templár, to trim the sails to the wind.

Temporál, storm.
Tenedéro, gripe or hold of an anchor.
Tenedéro (fóndo de buén), good anchoring-ground.
Tenedór de bastiméntos, store-keeper of the navy.
Tenedúria, naval store-house.
Tesár, to stretch out, to haul taut.
Tesár la járcia, to set up.
Téso, taut-hauled, tight.
Tiémpo, weather.
Tiémpo cargádo ó gruéso, thick, hazy weather.
Tiémpo borrascóso, stormy weather.
Tiémpo de juanétes, topgallant gale.
Tiénda, awning.
Tiérra, land.
Tiérra á tiérra, to sail close in-shore.
Timón, helm, rudder.
Timón (la mádre del), the mainpiece of the rudder.
Timón (el azafrán del), the afterpiece of the rudder.
Timón (la cabéza del), the rudder-head.
Timón (la mortája del), the mortise of the rudder.
Timón (fórro del), the back of the rudder.
Timón (sacár ó apeár el), to unship the rudder.
Timón (calár el), to hang the rudder.
Timoneár, to steer, to govern the helm.
Timonél ó Timonéro, steersman, helmsman.
Tíra, fall, running.
Tíra de un aparéjo, fall of a tackle.
Tíra de un aparéjo reál, a winding tackle-fall.
Tíra del aparéjo de la gáta, the cat-tackle fall.
Tíra de las aparejuélas de pórtas, port-tackle fall.
Tirámollár, to overhaul, to ease off, to lower.
Tíramollár las amúras y escótas, to overhaul the
    sheets and tacks.
Tocár, to shake, to shiver, to touch.
Togíno, notch or knob to secure things from moving.

Tojínes, cleats.
Tojínes de las vérgas, cleats of the yards.
Tojíno de tojíno, cleat and cleat.
Toldílla, poop.
Tóldo, awning.
Tóldo del castíllo, forecastle-awning.
Tóldo del alcázar, quarter-deck-awning.
Tóldo de pópa, poop or after-awning.
Tóldo de inviérno, weather-cloth.
Tóldo del cómbes, main-deck-awning.
Tóldos (candeléros de los), stanchions of the awnings.
Toléte, pin of a boat, thole.
Tomadóres, furling lines, gaskets, rope-bands.
Tomadóres de la crúz, bunt gaskets.
Tomadóres del tércio, quarter gaskets.
Tomadóres de los fenóles, yardarm gaskets.
Tomár, to take.
Tomár por avánte, to take aback.
Tomár viénto, to trim the sails to the wind.
Tomár puérto, to go into port.
Tonelada, ton.
Tonelage, tonnage.
Tópe, top, lookout.
Tópe de un tablón, butt-end of a plank.
Tópe de la arboladúra, masthead.
Tormentín, a small mast on the bowsprit.
Tormentóso, a stiff vessel, a vessel apt to be dismasted.
Tórre de lúces, lighthouse.
Tortór, lashing, fraps.
Tortór (pálo de), Spanish windlass.
Tortóres (dár tortóres á un búque), to frap a ship.
Trabáculo, Austrian trabacolo.
Tráca, strake, the range of planking of a vessel.
Tráca de palmejáres, strake of the ceiling or foot-waling.
Tragadéro de un puérto, the entrance of a harbour.

Tragadéro (estár en el tragadéro del már), to be in the trough of the sea.

Tragánte, pump.

Tragánte del bauprés, pillow of the bowsprit.

Tragánte de pedréro, stock or crotche of a swivel gun.

Tráma, weft, shoot.

Trancaníles, water-ways.

Trancaníles reservádos ó interióres, under-water-ways.

Transbordár, to tranship.

Transpórte, transport.

Trápas, spilling-lines, relieving-ropes.

Trasbuchár, to gybe, to shift.

Travérsa, backstay.

Través (al, de, por el), abreast the beam, abeam, athwart ship, across ship.

Través (por la próa del), before the beam.

Través (por la pópa del), abaft the beam.

Través (por el través de las bárbas) athwart hawse.

Través (viénto por el), wind on the beam.

Travesía, passage, voyage, side-wind.

Trazár, to draw a plan.

Trazár practicaménte, practical sail cutting.

Tréo, scudding-sail, square-sail, cross-jack-sail.

Trínca, any cord that serves to lash or make fast.

Trínca (á la), close-hauled.

Trincádo, tringuard.

Trincadúra, Biscayan lugger.

Trincafía, marlinghitch, closehitch, a kind of knot.

Trincafiár, to marl, to fix.

Tríncas, seizings.

Tríncas del bauprés, gammoning of the bowsprit.

Trincár, to keep close to the wind.

Trincár los cábos, to fasten the rope-ends.

Trincar las puértas, to bar in the port-lids.

Trinquéte, foresail, fore-course, foremast.

Trinquéte con botalón, boom-foresail.
Trinquéte cangréjo, fore-spencer.
Trinquetílla, fore-staysail.
Tripulacion, crew of a ship.
Tripuládo, manned, equipped.
Tríza, cord, rope.
Trocéo ó Tróza, truss, parrel.
Tronéra, loop-hole.
Trozéo, a rope that holds the yard to the mast.
Trózo, junk, pieces of old cables for making oakum.
Tumbár, to shift, to heel, to lie along.
Tumbár un búque, to heave a ship down.

U

Uracán, hurricane.
Urca, hooker, dogger, sloop-rigged vessel, store-ship.
Urdido ó Urdímbre, warp, chain.
Urnición, top-timbers.
Ustága, tie.

V

Vaína, tabling, table.
Vaína del gratíl, head-tabling.
Vaína del pujámen, foot-tabling.
Vaína de la valúma, leech-tabling.
Vaína de bandéra, hoist of a flag, edging.
Vaivén, rattling-line.
Valíza, beacon, buoy, a mark indicating some danger.
Valúma, leech, after-leech.
Varadéros, skids or skeeds.

Varadór, voyal, a hawser to help the heaving-in of the anchor.

Varár, to launch a vessel, to ground, to run ashore.

Varénga, floor-timber.

Varénga de plán, midship floor-timber.

Varénga de sobreplános, floor-rider.

Varengáge, a collection of floor-timbers.

Varón, head-line.

Varón del timón, rudder-pendant.

Véla, sail.

Véla cuádra, squaresail.

Véla latína, lateensail.

Véla de cuchíllo, fore-and-aft sail, trapezoid sail.

Véla mística, lugsail.

Véla guáyra, sliding-guntersail.

Véla de abaníco, spritsail.

Véla tarquína, lugsail.

Véla al tércio, lugsail.

Véla de cóncha, convergent sail.

Véla en sáco, unfinished sails without the tabling.

Véla envaináda, tabled sail.

Véla espigáda, very sharp-angled lateensail.

Véla faldóna, slack sail.

Véla de estái, staysail.

Véla de estái mayór, main-staysail.

Véla de estái de gávia, maintopmast-staysail.

Véla de estái dè juanéte mayór, maintopgallant-staysail

Véla de estái volánte, middle-staysail.

Véla de estái de mesána, mizen-staysail.

Véla de estái de sobremesána, mizen-topmast staysail.

Véla de estái de periquíto, mizen-topmast staysail.

Véla de fortúna, trysail, stormsail.

Véla de pópa, aft-sail.

Véla mayór, mainsail.

Véla del trinquéte, foresail.

Véla de mesána, mizen.
Véla de gávia, main-topsail.
Véla de velácho, fore-topsail.
Véla de sobremesána, mizen-topsail.
Véla de juanéte mayór, main-topgallantsail.
Véla de juanéte de próa, fore-topgallantsail.
Véla de periquíto de sobremesána, mizen-topgallantsail
Véla de cebadéra, spritsail.
Véla de sobrecebadéra, spritsail-topsail.
Véla séca, cross-jacksail.
Véla de mericangállo, driver.
Véla de sénda, trysail.
Véla de cangréja, boomsail.
Vélas de próa, foresails, head-sails.
Vélas áltas, upper sails.
Vélas bájas, lower sails.
Vélas menúdas, flying-sails.
Vélas de respéto, store-sails.
Vélas mayóres, courses.
Véla barredéra, drabler.
Véla de crúz, a square-sail.
Véla de lastrár, portsail.
Véla (caída de una), drop or depth of a sail.
Véla (gratíl de una), head of a sail.
Véla encapilláda, sail blown over the yard.
Véla aferráda, a furled sail.
Véla cazáda, trimmed sail.
Véla lárga ó desaferráda, unfurled sail.
Véla cargáda arríba, a sail hauled up in the brails.
Véla tendída, taut or full sail.
Véla desrelingáda, sail blown from the bolt-rope.
Véla en fácha, backed sail.
Véla que flaméa, a sail shivering in the wind.
Véla (marcár una), to set a sail.
Véla (hacérse á la), to set sail, to leave port.

Velachéro, polacre-settee, a small craft used in the Mediterranean.
Velácho, fore-topsail.
Velámen, sails, canvas, set of sails.
Velár las escótas, to stand by the sheets.
Velejár, to make use of sails.
Veléro, sailmaker.
Ventarrón, strong gale.
Venteár, to blow very fresh.
Ventiladór, windsail.
Ventolínas, baffling winds, light airs, light wind.
Vérga, yard.
Vérga mayór, mainyard.
Vérga de trinquéte, foreyard.
Vérga séca, cross-jackyard.
Vérga de gávia, maintopsail-yard.
Vérga de velácho, foretopsail-yard.
Vérga de sobremesána, mizentopsail-yard.
Vérga de juanéte, maintopsail-yard.
Vérga de juanéte de próa, foretopgallant-yard.
Vérga de juanéte sobremesána, mizentopgallant-yard.
Vérga de sobrejuanéte mayór, mainroyal-yard.
Vérga de sobrejuanéte de próa, foreroyal-yard.
Vérga de sobreperiquíto, mizenroyal-yard.
Vérga de aparéjo de abaníco, sprit.
Vérga de ála, studdingsail-yard.
Vérga de cebadéra, spritsail-yard.
Vérgas (ponér las vérgas en crúz), to square the yards.
Vertedór, a scoop used to throw the water out of boats.
Vertéllos, trucks.
Viénto, guy.
Viénto, wind.
Viénto flójo, light breeze.
Viénto fresquíto, fresh breeze
Viénto bonancíble, moderate breeze.

Viénto frésco, strong breeze.
Viénto frescachón, moderate gale.
Viénto dúro, fresh gale.
Viénto lárgo, large wind, leading wind.
Viénto á la cuádra, side wind.
Viénto al través, side wind, on the beam, before the beam
Viénto por la pópa, stern wind, wind aft.
Viénto por la próa, head wind, wind ahead.
Viénto por la aléta, quarterly wind, booming.
Viénto por la amúra, bow wind.
Viénto de bolína, sharp wind.
Viénto á fil de róda, wind right ahead, heaving in stays.
Viénto favoráble, fair wind.
Viénto (orígen del), wind's eye.
Viénto contrário, foul wind.
Viénto galérno; a fresh wind.
Viénto derrotéro, wind on the beam, trade wind.
Vigía, the look-out.
Vigiár, to look out, to watch.
Vigóta, dead-eye.
Viguería, all the beams, the timber-work of a ship.
Vinatéras, beckets.
Viquitórtes, quarter-gallery knees.
Viráda, going or veering about, tacking, tack.
Viráda (faltár la), to miss stays.
Viradór, toprope.
Viradór de cubiérta, voyal.
Virár, to go about, to go round, to tack.
Víta, cross-beam on the forecastle.
Vítre, thin canvas, duck.
Voceár á un bajél, to hail a ship.
Vocína, speaking-trumpet.
Volánte, shifting, preventer.
Volár, to let go, to let fly.
Voleár, to overset a vessel.

Vuélo, fly.
Vuélta, board.
Vuélta redónda, to chapel or chapelling.

Y

Yac ó Yate, yacht.
Yúgo de la caña, counter-transom.
Yúgo de la cubiérta, deck-transom.
Yúgo principál, wing-transom.
Yúgo, transom.

Z

Zabordamiénto ó Zabórda, the stranding of a ship.
Zabordár, to strand, to run ashore, to ground.
Zábra, a small vessel used on the coast of Biscay.
Zafarráncho, hammock.
Zafarráncho (hacér el); clearing of the ship for action.
Zafárse, to haul off.
Zafár, to lighten a ship.
Zafárse de los bájos, to get clear of the shoals.
Zallár, to rouse.
Zalomár, to sing out.
Zancadílla, elbow in the hawse.
Zánco, flagstaff.
Zapáta de un áncla, shoe of an anchor.
Zapáta de la quílla, the false keel.
Zarpár, to weigh anchor.
Zarpár (el áncla está zarpádo), the anchor is a-trip.
Zayár, to hawse, to haul a tackle.
Zínga, a watch, a day's run.
Zoquéte de cuchára, scoop-handle.
Zozobrár, to capsize, to upset, to overset.
Zúncho, hoop.

ENGLISH AND SPANISH.

ABA—AFT

Aback, en fácha.

Aback (to brace), abroquelár, ponérse en fácha, ponér las vélas en fácha.

Abaft, á pópa ó en pópa.

Abeam, á la cuádra ó por la cuádra.

Aboard, á bórdo.

Aboard a ship (to fall), abordár un navío.

About (to go), virár.

Acorn, perílla.

Adjustment (average), arréglo de avéria gruésa.

Admiral, almiránte.

Admiral (rear), contraalmírante ó géfe de escuádra.

Admiralty, almírantázgo.

Adrift (to go), abatír, flotár á mercéd de las águas.

Advice-boat, bajél de avíso, patáche.

Afloat, á flote, flotánte.

Afore, á proa.

Aft, popél, á pópa, hácia la pópa, por la pópa.

Aft (fore-and), de pópa á próa, de próa á pópa.

Aft (to haul the mizen-sheet close), cazár del tódo la escóta de mesána.

After-end, péna.

After-leechrope, relónga de la caída de pópa.

Aftermost, el último, él de mas atrás.

Aft-part, Aft-side, cara de pópa.

Aft-sails, vélas de pópa.

After-sails, aparéjo mayór.

G

Aground, barádo, encalládo, á la pláya, enbancádo.

Ahead, por la próa.

Airs, ayres.

Airs (light), ventolínas.

Aloft, arríba.

Aloft (all hands), todo el múndo arríba.

Alongside (to lay), abarloár, atracár.

Anemometer, anemómetro, un instruménto para medír la presíon del viénto sobre una superficíe dáda.

Anchor (lying at), súrto, al áncla, ancládo.

Anchor-arm, úñas del áncla.

Anchor-back, gálga del áncla.

Anchor-bill, píco del áncla.

Anchor-cross, crúz del áncla.

Anchor-forge, ancoretía.

Anchor-flukes, oréjas del áncla.

Anchor-ring, argáneo, argólla.

Anchor-smith, ancoréro.

Anchor (best bower), áncla de ayúste.

Anchor (small bower), áncla sencílla.

Anchor (sheet), anclóte ó áncla de esperánza.

Anchor-shank, caña del áncla.

Anchor-stock, cépo del áncla.

Anchor (to stock the), encepár el áncla.

Anchor-ground, fondeadéro, agarradéro, ancláge.

Anchorage, ancláge, fondeadéro, agarradéro.

Anchoring, agarradéro, fondeadéro.

Apron of the stem, albitána ó contraróda.

Arm (to), armár.

Arm (lee), péna.

Arm (yard), pénol.

At the water edge, á flor de água.

Athwart ship, de babór en estribór, por la cuádra.

Athwart (to set), atravesárse.

Avast heaving, fórte, bastá, no más.

Average, avería.
Average (general), avería gruésa.
Away (to keep), amollár.
Aweather, barlovénto.
Awning, tóldo.
Awning (forecastle), tóldo de castíllo.
Awning (after, poop awning), tóldo de pópa.
Awning (quarter-deck), tóldo de alcazár.
Awning-stanchions, candeléros de los tóldos.
Axle-tree, pérno de roldána.

B

Back, gálga de áncla.
Back a-stern (to), ciár.
Back-board, escúdo de bóte, respáldo.
Backstay, brandál.
Backstays (shifting), brandáles volántes.
Back-stitch, pespúnte.
Back (to back the sails), braceár en fácha.
Back (to back-stitch), pespúntar.
Backstay-stools, mesétas de los brandáles.
Bag-reef, rízos chícos.
Balance-reef, antagálla.
Balance (to), antagallár.
Ballast, enjúnque, lástre.
Ballast (to), enjuncár ó hacér enjúnque, lastrár.
Ballast (to go in), ír en lástre.
Ballast (washed), guijárro, ó lástre lavádo.
Ballast-lighter, lanchón de delastrár.
Ballast-ports, pórtas de lastrár.
Band, esterílla, fája.
Band (to), fajeár.

Band (foot), fája de pié.
Band (middle or strengthening), fája de médio.
Band (iron), súncho.
Barge, falúa.
Barque, bárca.
Bastard, bastárdo, nombre de una véla.
Beam (on the), por el través, á la cuádra.
Beam (abreast the, a-), al través, por el través.
Beam (before the), por la próa del través.
Beams (to fill up the), abarrotár.
Beams, báos.
Beams of the upper decks, báos de las cubiértas altas.
Beam (aftermost), báo popéro.
Beam (foremost), báo proél.
Beam (midship), báo maéstro.
Beam (abaft the), por la pópa del través.
Bear away (to), to bear down, to bear up, arribár.
Bear (to bear away large), navegár arribádo ó arribár
       á escóta lárga.
Bear (to bear away before the wind), arribár todo.
Beat to windward (to), barloventeár.
Becket, binatéra.
Belaying-cleat, cornamúsa, escotéra.
Belaying-pin, cavílla.
Belay a rope (to), amarrár ó dar vuélta á un cábo.
Belay (to belay a running rope), amarrár un cábo de labor
Belee (to), sotaventár.
Belly, barríga.
Belly or bag-part of a sail, sáco.
Belly of a sail, bólsos.
Bend, núdo.
Bend (to), ayustár ó envergár.
Bend (the), ayúste.
Beneaped, barrádo, encalládo.
Bermudoe-sail, aúrica, cangréja.

Berth, el sítio adonde se colóca un búque en un dique ó puérto.

Between decks, entrepuéntes.

Between ports, cháza.

Between wind and water, entre dos águas.

Bight, séno.

Bill of lading, conocimiénto.

Bill of the ánchor, píco del áncla.

Binnacle or Bittacle, bitácora.

Binding-streaks, cuérdas ó eslóras.

Bit (to), tomár la bitadúra con un cáble.

Bit of a cable, bitadúra del cáble.

Bits (topsail), abitónes.

Bits (lining of the), fórro de las bítas.

Bitts or bits, bítas.

Block or single block, motón, cuadernál, poléa.

Block-mast, pálo mácho.

Block (tie), motón de palóma.

Block (tail), motón de rabíza.

Block (large), tálla.

Block and block, á besár.

Bluff-bowed ship, búque de muchos llénos.

Board, vuélta, puénte.

Board (serving), paléta de ferrár.

Board, bordáda.

Board (to), abordár.

Board (to make a good), barloventeár bién.

Board (on), á bordo.

Boarding a ship (the), abordáje.

Boarding-axes, achuélas de abordáje.

Boat, bóte, embarcación menór.

Boat (advice), avíso.

Boat (an Italian fishing), balancéla.

Boat (bermudoe-rigged), pailebót.

Boat (watering), aljibe.

Boat's cloth, empavesáda de bóte.

Boat-hook, bichéro.

Boat (shipwright's), bóte de maestránza.

Boat (pilot's), pailebót.

Boat-rope, bóza, cordél de bóte.

Boatswain, contramaéstre.

Bobstay, barbiquéjo, freníllo.

Bobstay-holes, gruéras de tajamár.

Body of the ship, casco.

Bollards, estácas de díque.

Bollard-timbers, guindástes.

Bolster, almoháda de los pálos.

Bolt, pérno.

Bolt-rope, relínga.

Bombarder, bombárda.

Bonnet, bonéta.

Book (log), cuadérno de bitácora.

Boom, botalón.

Boom-irons, súnchos de los botalónes.

Boom-foresail, trinquéte con botalón.

Boom (jib), batallól, batalón de fóque.

Boom (lower studdingsail), tangón.

Boomkin, pescánte de la amúra del trinquéte.

Boom-tackle, escóta de la botavára.

Boom-saddle, descánso.

Booming-wind, viénto por la aléta.

Bottom, fóndo.

Bottomry, dinéro á la gruésa, cásco y quílla, hipóteca.

Bow, cachéte, amúra, próa,

Bow (on the), por la amúra, por la servióla.

Bowline, bolína.

Bowlines (to haul the), bolineár.

Bowline-cringle, garrúcho de la próa de bolína.

Bowline-tackle, aparéjo de bolineár.

Bowlines (bridles of the), póas.

Bowline (on the taut), navegár á bolína agarrocháda.
Bow-wind, viénto por la amúra.
Bower-anchor, áncla de servidúmbre.
Bowsprit, pálo bauprés, bauprés.
Bowsprit-shrouds, mostáchos.
Box (to box off), abroquelár.
Brace, bráza.
Brace (lateen), orzapópa, óstas.
Brace (to), braceár.
Brace (to brace aback), abroquelár.
Brace sharp up (to), braceár á ceñir, braceár en cája.
Braces of a rudder, hémbras del timón.
Bracing (the), bracéo.
Brackets (cat-head), alétas de las serviólas.
Brails, brióles, candalízas, cargadéras.
Brake, guimbaléte de bómba.
Breadth (main), firme.
Breadth of a ship, mánga de un búque.
Break (to), faltár, desbaratár.
Breastfast, amárra del través.
Breast-hooks, buzárdas.
Breast-rail, antepécho.
Breast-rope, guardamancébo.
Breechings, braguéros de cañon.
Breem (to), quemár el fóndo de un búque, para limpiárlo
Breeze (light), viénto flójo.
Breeze (fresh), viénto fresquíto.
Breeze (moderate), viénto bonancíble.
Breeze (strong), viénto frésco.
Bridles of the bowlines, póas.
Bridle the oars (to), acorullár.
Brig, bergantín.
Brig (schooner brig-rigged forward), bergantín goléta.
Bring to (to), facheár, ponérse á la cápa.
Bring up (to), orzár.

Broad pendant, cornéta.
Broad seams, péjes.
Broadside, andanáda.
Brokerage, corretáje.
Bruise-water or old tub, un cascarón.
Builder's certificate, certificádo de propiedád.
Bulkheads, mámparos.
Bulge, abertúra de água.
Bull's-eye, bertéllo, ójo de buéy ú ójo de ciégo.
Bulwark, batayóla, obra muérta.
Bumboat, bóte vivandéro.
Bumkin, pescánte de la amúra del trinquéte.
Bunt, martíllo, barríga, braguéro.
Bunt-gaskets, tomadóres de la crúz.
Buntlines, brióles del pujámen.
Buntline cloths, refuérzos de los brióles.
Bunt of a sail, camiséta, batidéro de véla.
Bunting, lanílla.
Buoy, bóya.
Buoy (can-buoy), bóya coníca.
Buoy-rope, orínque.
Buoy-slings, eslíngas de bóya.
Buoy (to buoy the cable), boyár el cáble.
Burden, pórte.
Burton, aparéjo de poléa, aparéjo.
Buttock, llénos de la pópa, la parte entre el yúgo
    principál y la linéa superiór del água.

C

Cabin, cámara ó camaróte.
Cabin-boy, mózo de cámara, muchácho de cámara,
    páje de escóba.
Cable, cáble.

Cable (best bower), cáble del ayúste.
Cable (small bower), cáble sencíllo ó de léva.
Cable (sheet), cáble de esperánza.
Cable (stream), calabróte.
Cable-bit, bitadúra ó média bitadúra.
Cable (weather-bit of a), bitadúra entéra de cáble.
Cable (to bit the), tomár la bitadúra con el cáble.
Cable (to serve the), aferrár el cáble.
Cable (to slip the), alargár el cáble.
Cablet, calabróte.
Caburns, cajétas.
Caic or Caique, caíque, una pequeña embarcación de úso en el már négro.
Calm, cálma.
Calm (dead), cálma muérta, cálma chícha.
Callipers, compás cúrbo.
Camber, tablón con vuélta circulár.
Cambered-deck, puénte combádo.
Camel, una espécie de bárco.
Can-buoy, bóya conica de barríl.
Can-hooks, gáfas.
Cannon-hole, tronéra.
Cant-frames, cuadérnas reverádas.
Canvas, lóna, velámen.
Canvas (thin), vitre.
Canvas-hose, manguéra.
Cap, tamboréte, capíllo.
Caps (holes in the caps to allow the masts to pass through), bóca de tinája.
Capsize (to), zozobrár, trabucár.
Capsquares, sobremuñonéras.
Capstan or Capstern, cabrestánte.
Capstan-barrel, cuérpo del cabrestánte.
Capstan-whelps, guardainfántes.
Capstan-chocks, cúñas de cabrestánte.

Capstan-drumhead, cabéza de cabrestánte.
Capstan-spindle, pínola del cabrestánte.
Capstan (step of the), cóncha ó carlínga del cabrestánte.
Capstan-bars, bárras del cabrestánte.
Capstan-pins, perníllos del cabrestánte.
Capstan (to rig the), guarnir el cabrestánte.
Capstan (to paul the), pasár lingüéte.
Captain, capitán.
Captain of the top, gaviéro mayór.
Carcass of a vessel, cásco de úna embarcación.
Careen, caréna.
Careen (to), carenár.
Careening-gear, aparéjo de carenár.
Careening-wharf, muélle de carenáge.
Cargo, cargaménto.
Carlings, atravesáños.
Carlings of the hatchways, galeótas de las escotíllas.
Carry (to), portár.
Carriage by sea, transpórte.
Case (to), aferrár.
Cased mats, afelpádos.
Casks or gang-casks, pipería.
Caskets, tomadóres.
Casting, caída del búque.
Cathead, servióla.
Cathook, gáncho de la gáta.
Cattackle, aparéjo de gáta.
Catharpings or Catharpins, jarétas.
Catspaws, ayrecítos, sóplos.
Catch, cuaíche, nómbre de una embarcación.
Caulk (to), calafateár ó calfateár.
Caulking-iron, escóplo de calafáte.
Caulking-mallet, macéta de calafáte.
Chafe (to), rozár, luír, mascárse.
Chafing, rozadúra.

Chain, cadéna, urdído, urdímbre.
Chain-necklaces, súncho de las arraigádas.
Chain-wale, mésa de guarnícion.
Chain-plates, cadénas de las vigótas.
Chains (top), cadénas de las vérgas.
Channel, mésa de guarnícion, ranúra.
Channel-truck, bertéllo de canál.
Channel of a block, cajéra.
Channels (fire), canáles de fuégo.
Chapel (to), dar vuélta redónda.
Chapelling, tomár por la lúa.
Chart, cárta de navegár ó de mareár.
Charter-party, contráta de fletamiénto.
Chase (to), cazár.
Chase (stern), guardatimónes.
Chasing-jib, fóque de cáza.
Check, sálto, lascón.
Check (to), saltár.
Cheeks, cachétes, cachólas.
Cheeks of the head, gantéras, tajamár.
Check of the pump, picóta.
Chess-trees, galápagos ó castañuélas de las amúras.
Chinse (to), calafateár.
Chocks, cálzos, cúñas de madéra.
Clapper, chapeléta de la bómba.
Claw, páta de gánso, pié de cábra, úñas de espéque.
Cleat, tojíno, tojíno de vérga, galápago de las palómas.
Cleat-and-cleat, tojíno de tojíno.
Clinching, solapadúra, un calfatéo superficial.
Close-home, á besár.
Close-hauled, búque ceñído.
Close-reef, rízos chicos.
Close-work, punto de telár.
Cloth (top), batidéro.
Cloth, páño.

Cloth (gored, goring-cloth), páño de brúsca.
Cloth (square), páño cuadrádo.
Cloth (leech), paño de cuchíllo.
Cloth (head), páño del gratíl.
Cloth (foot), páño del pujámen.
Cloth (weather), tóldo de inviérno.
Cloth (sail), lóna, velámen.
Clue or Clew, púño, púño de la escóta.
Clue-garnet, palanquín, chafaldéte ó cargapúños.
Clue-line, chafaldétes de los púños.
Clue-rope, relónga del páño.
Clues, púños bájos.
Coaster, patáche, búque de cabotáje, costéro.
Coat, fúnda.
Coasting trade, cabotáje.
Cobbing-board, paléta de azotár.
Cock-boat, bóte de navío.
Cockswain, patrón de bóte.
Cockpit, entarimádo del solládo.
Coil, adúja, rollo, adujáda.
Coil (to coil a cable), adujár un cáble.
Collar, collár, encapilladúra.
Collier or coal vessel, carbonéro.
Colors (to hoist the), enarbolár la bandéra.
Combings of the hatches, brazólas.
Combings of hemp, brín.
Come to the wind (to), aproár al viénto.
Coming to, coming up, orzáda.
Companion, carróza.
Company, dotación, equipáge, tripulación.
Compass (point of the), rúmbo.
Compass, compás de már, brújula, agúja de mareár.
Compass (azimuth), brújula de azímut.
Compass (hanging), brújula reviráda de cámara.
Compass-timber, madéra de vuélta.

Concentrated jib, fóque de abaníco ó fóque de cóncha.

Concentrated sail or convergent sail, véla de cóncha ó véla de abaníco.

Connexion, ligazón.

Cordage, járcia, cordáge, conjúnto de cábos.

Corner, capuchíno.

Corner-pieces, dádos.

Corposant, fuégo de santelmo.

Cot, hamáca.

Cot-bottom, cátre.

Counter, bovedílla superiór.

Counter-tide, contramaréa.

Course, rúmbo.

Course (fore), trinquéte.

Course (main), mayór redónda.

Courses, mayóres.

Cove, caléta, ensenáda.

Covering, fúnda.

Crab, cabrestánte sencíllo ó volánte.

Cradle, cúna; canál que sírve para guiár un búque cuándó se bóta al água de los astilléros.

Craft, nómbre generíco para toda embarcación, pero principalménte applicádo á los menóres. .

Craft (small), búque de cabotáje.

Crane, pescánte.

Crank, manúbrio, ciqueñál, enciqueñádo.

Crank-pin, pérno del ciqueñál.

Crank ship, búque fálso, búque celóso.

Crank-sided vessel, búque celóso que túmba á la bánda y no aguánta véla.

Crease (to), amoldár, señalár.

Creasing of the seam, dobléz.

Creek, cála, caléta, ensenáda.

Crew of a vessel, tripulación, dotación, el número de marinéros á bórdo.

Cringle, garrúcho.

Cringle (clue), garrúcho del púño de la escóta.

Cringle (reef-tackle), púños de las pájas.

Cringle (bowline), garrúcho de la póa de bolína.

Cross-bar-shot, palanquéta.

Crosspiece of the bits, crúz de las bítas.

Crosspiece of the forecastle, atravesáño del propáo del castíllo.

Cross-staff, ballestílla.

Cross-gore, áspa, diagonál.

Cross-jack, véla séca.

Cross-jacksail, mesána redónda.

Cross-jack-yard, vérga séca.

Cross-stitch, púntos cruzádos, lláves.

Cross-trees, crucétas de la cófa.

Crotche, candeléro, horquéta.

Crow-foot, aráña.

Crowd (to crowd sail), hacér fuérza de véla.

Crown of the anchor, crúz del áncla.

Cruise, córso, un viáge de placér, un viáge de observación en tiémpo de guérra, sin rúmbo fijo.

Cuddy, carróza de bárco abiérto.

Curtains, cenéfas.

Cut away (to), derríbar.

Cutter, balándra, segúndo bóte.

Cutting-down (the), astílla muérta.

Cutting-down líne, arrúfo de astílla muérta.

Cut-water, tajamár.

Cut-water (beak of the), espolón del tajámár.

Cut-water (fore-piece of the), azafrán del tajamár.

Cut-water (doublings of the), batidóres de próa.

D

Damage avería.

Dark, abromádo, nebulóso.

Davit, pescánte de áncla.

Days (lay), días de pláncha.

Deaden (to), amortiguár.

Dead-block, cuadérnal ciégo.

Dead-eyes, vigótas, motónes chátos sin roldánas.

Dead-lights, postígos ó portas de corrér, colocádas en las ventánas de pópa.

Dead-reckoning, estíma de la posición del búque por el log ó la barquílla y corredéra, sin observación astronomíca.

Dead-rising (the), astílla muérta.

Dead-rising, linéa del arrúfo del cuérpo principál.

Dead-water, estéla, águas muértas ó revéses de las águas de un búque.

Dead-work, óbrá muérta.

Dead-wood, dormídos.

Deck, cubiérta.

Deck (quarter), alcazár.

Decks (between), entrepuéntes.

Decked-vessel, búque de cubiérta corrída.

Deep-sea-line, escandállo ó sónda.

Demurrage, días de demóra.

Depth, caída de fuéra.

Depth in the hold, puntál.

Depth of a vessel, puntál de un búque.

Diamond-pieces, dádos.

Dinnage or dunnage, madéras que se póne debájo de la cárga, para conservár las táblas del búque y la cárga.

Dismast (to), desarbolár.

Dismasted (to be), sufrír un desarbólo.

Dŏck, díque
Dock (dry), díque séco, atarazána, astilléro.
Dock (floating), díque flotánte.
Dock-yard, astilléro, arsenál.
Dock (to), ponér un búque en el díque.
Dogger, bárca de pescadór.
Dog-vane, cataviénto.
Dolphin-striker, móco.
Donkey-engine, máquina alimentícia.
Double (to double a cape), montár ó doblár un cábo
     ó promontório.
Double (to double a ship's bottom), embonár.
Doubling of the bits, almohádas de las bítas.
Doubling of a ship's bottom, embón, refuérzo del
     fóndo de un búque.
Doubling of the cut-water, batidéros de próa.
Down-haul, cargadéra, rabíza de bandéra.
Downhaul-tackle, aparéjo de cargadéra.
Drabler, bonéta, véla barredéra.
Draft or Draught, caládo.
Drag the anchor (to), arancár el áncla.
Draught (sailing), en buénas águas.
Draught-hooks of a gun-carriage, argóllas de curéña.
Draw up (to), izár.
Draw down (to), arriár, lascár.
Dress (to), empavesár.
Drift, deríva.
Drive (to), arronzár, derivár.
Drive (to drive to leeward), sotaventeár.
Driver, mesána, maricangálla.
Driver-boom, botavára, botalón de maricangálla.
Driving-fid, burél.
Drop, caída al céntro, caída de fuéra.
Duck or Russian duck, liénzo de Rúsia.
Duck (raven's), lonéta.

E

Ear, empuñidúra.
Earing, púño del gratíl, empuñidúra.
Earing of a sail, empuñidúra de una véla.
Earing-splice, ójo.
Earings, púños áltos.
Earings (head), empuñidúras del gratíl.
Earings (reef), empuñidúras de rízos.
Ease off (to), tiramollár, lascár, arriár.
Ease (to), arriár, lascár.
Ease (to ease the ship), orzár tódo.
Ease the shrouds (to), aflojár los obénques.
Eating-in, embebído.
Eating in seaming, brúsca de costúra.
Ebb, menguánte, maréa bája.
Ebb-anchor, áncla del menguánte.
Ebb-tide, maréa menguánte.
Eddy of the tide, revéses de la maréa.
Eddy-water, estéla, água muérta.
Edge, lómo.
Edge (to edge away), inclinárse á sotavénto.
Edge of a cloth, orílla.
Edging, vaína de bandéra.
End-for-end, de chicóte á chicóte.
End of a rope, chicóte.
End (after), péna.
Ensign, bandéra de pópa.
Ensign-halliard. dríza de bandéra.
Entáckle, aparejár.
Enter the mouth of a channel (to), abocár un estrécho.
Entering-rope, guardamancébo.
Equipment, armaménto.
Escutcheon, espéjo.
Estimate-memorial, presupuésto.

H

Eye-bolts, cáncamos del ójo.
Eyelet-holes of the reefs, olláos de rízos
Eye-splice, gáza, ójo.

F

Fag-end, cordón.
Fail (to), mancár.
Fake, adúja de cáble.
Fall, tíra.
Fall of a tackle, tíra de aparéjo.
Fall off from the wind (to), arribár.
Fall (to fall aboard), abordár, caér sobre un bajél.
Fall (to fall astern), dejárse caér por la pópa.
Fall (to fall calm), calmár.
Fall (to fall to leeward), dejárse caér á sotavénto.
Falling-home vessel, búque abiérto de bócas.
Falling-off vessel, caída del búque, arribáda.
Fan, abaníco.
Fashion-pieces, alétas.
Fast-sailing vessel (a), búque veléro.
Fast (to), ayustár.
Fast (the), ayúste.
Fastening, encapilladúra.
Fasts, amárras.
Fathom (to), abrazár, sondár.
Fay (to), escaraboteár, ayustár una piéza con otra.
Feather-vane, cataviénto.
Feaze (to), destorcér el chicóte de un cábo.
Felucca, falúa.
Felucco, falúcho.
Ferry-boat, bóte de pasáje.
Fetch (to fetch away), tenér juégo.
Fetch (to fetch the pump), llamár la bómba.
Fid, pasadór, burél.

Fid of a topmast, cúña de masteléro.

Fid-hole, ójo de la cúña de masteléro.

Fill (to), mareár.

Fill the sails (to), braceár en viénto.

Fin (to), encapillár.

First-jib, fóque gránde.

Fish, gimélga.

Fish of an anchor, pescánte de áncla.

Fish-spear, arpón, dárdo.

Fish-tackle, aparéjo de pescánte.

Fit (to), aparejár. .

Fit out (to), armár.

Fitting out (the), armaménto.

Fix (to), trincafiár.

Flag, bandéra.

Flag (hoist of a), váina de bandéra.

Flag (distinguishing), insígnia.

Flag (merchant), bandéra mercánte.

Flag (national), bandéra de guérra.

Flag (signal), bandéra de señáles.

Flag (tack of a), relónga de bandéra.

Flag-halliard, dríza de bandéra.

Flag-officer, bandéra cuádra ó de insígnia; oficiál de marína que mánda una escuádra.

Flag-ship, navío almiránte.

Flag-staff, el ásta de una bandéra.

Flat of an oar, pála de rémo.

Flat of a floor-timber, plán de una varénga.

Flat (to flat in), acuartelár, abroquelár.

Flat-quarter, pópa llána.

Flatten (to), sobrecosér.

Floating-cistern, aljíbe.

Flood-anchor, áncla del creciénte.

Flook, lengüéta de áncora.

Floor-heads, maniguétes.

Floor of a ship, plán de un navío.
Floor-timbers, varéngas.
Flow, creciénte de la maréa.
Flowing-sheet, escóta aventáda.
Flukes of the anchor, oréjas del áncla.
Flush-decked ship, búque de cubiérta corrída.
Flutter, flameár.
Fly (to let fly the topgallant-sheets), volár las escótas de los juanétes.
Fly-boat, flibóte; una especíe de embarcación veléra.
Fly of an ensign, vuélo de úna bandéra.
Fly up (to), arribár en redóndo.
Flying-jib, petifóque.
Flying-jibboom, botalón de petifóque.
Flying-sails, vélas menúdas.
Flying-topgallantsail, juanéte volánte.
Foncet, foncéte.
Foot, pujámen.
Foot-band, fája de pié.
Foot-cloth, páño del pujámen.
Foot-gore, brúsca del pujámen.
Foot-lining, fája de pié.
Foot-rope, marchapié, relínga del pujámen.
Foot-tabling, váina del pujámen.
Fore part of a ship, proél, próa.
Fore or Afore, á próa.
Fore-and-aft, de pópa á próa.
Fore-and-aft sail, véla de cuchíllo.
Forecastle, castíllo.
Forecastle-awning, tóldo del castíllo.
Fore-course, tódo del castíllo.
Fore-foot, górja.
Fore-gears, dríza de la mayór.
Fore-leechrope, relónga de la caída de próa.
Fore-lock, chabéta.

Forelock-bolts, pérnos de chabéta.
Foremast, pálo de trinquéte.
Fore-part, hácia próa, por la próa, por la cára de próa.
Fore-reach (to), alcanzár y pasár otro navío.
Foresail, trinquéte.
Foresail (boom), trinquéte con botalón.
Foresails, vélas de próa.
Fore-sheet, escóta del trinquéte.
Fore-shrouds, obénques del trinquéte.
Fore-spencer, trinquéte cangréjo.
Forestaff, ballestílla, instruménto astronomíco.
Forestay, estái del trinquéte.
Forestay-tackle, candeletón.
Fore-staysail, trinquetílla.
Foretackle, aparéjo del gáncho del trinquéte.
Foretop, cofa del trinquéte.
Fore-topmast-staysail, contrafóque.
Fore-topsail-bowline, bolíche.
Fore-topgallantyard, vérga de juanéte de próa.
Fore-topsail, velácho.
Fore-topsailyard, vérga de velácho.
Fore-royalyard, vérga sobrejuanéte de próa.
Fore-yard, vérga de trinquéte.
Forward, hácia próa, por la próa, por la cára de próa.
Fox, rebénque, cajéta.
Founder (to), írse á píque.
Frame, bastidór, cuadérna.
Frame of a ship, armazón.
Frame-timbers, ligazónes.
Frame (midship), cuadérna maéstra.
Frame (stern), cuadérno del cuérpo de pópa.
Frames, brazádas.
Frames of a vessel, miémbros.
Free-board, obra muérta.
Free (sailing), navegár á un lárgo.

Freshes, avenídas.
Freshen (to), refrescár.
Fret, estrécho, brázo de már.
Friction-place, luchadéro ó luidéro.
Frigate-built or full-rigged, construcción de fragáta.
Frigate, fragáta.
Full (to keep), aparéjo lléno.
Full (to keep the sails), andár á buéna véla.
Full-rigged ship, fragáta mercánte.
Full and by, á buén viento.
Funnel, chimenéa.
Furl (to furl the sails), aferrár ó rifár las vélas.
Furl (to), empañicár.
Furling of a sail (the), rifadúra de una véla.
Furling-line, lanteón.
Furling-lines, tomadóres, aferravélas.
Furling-bands, aferravélas.

G

Gaff, pícos.
Gaff-boom, vérga de cangréja.
Gaffpeak-halliard, dríza del píco.
Gaff-sail, véla de cangréja.
Gaff-topgallantsail, sobre escandalósa.
Gaffthroat-halliard, driza de la bóca.
Gaff-topsail, escandalósa.
Gage, barlovénto.
Gage or Guage (to), arqueár, medír.
Gain (to gain the wind), ganár el barlovénto.
Gale (stiff), viénto récio ó fugáda récia.
Gale (to gale away), ír con viénto en pópa.
Gale (strong), ventarrón, temporál.
Gale (fresh), viénto dúro.
Gale (moderate), viénto frescachón.

Galleass, galeáza.
Galiot, galeóta.
Gall (to), rozár.
Gallery (quarter), jardín.
Gallery, corredór de navío.
Galley, galéra.
Gang, una partída de marinéros.
Gang-board, pláncha, andámio.
Gang-casks, pipería.
Gangway, corredór, pasamáno, portalón.
Garbel, aparadúra.
Garboard, táblas de la quílla.
Garland, rónda de ráncho.
Garnet, candeletón, estrínque.
Gasket, batafiél, matafión.
Gasket (awning), matafión de tóldo.
Gaskets, tomadóres.
Gaskets (bunt), tomadóres de la crúz.
Gaskets (quarter), tomadóres del tércio.
Gaskets (yardarm), tomadóres de los fenóles.
Gears, drízas.
Gears (main), drízas mayóres.
Gears (fore), drízas de la vérga del trinquéte.
Gear-block, cuadernál de palóma.
Gig, canóa.
Gimbals, balancínes de la brújula.
Girt, ména.
Girtline, andarivél.
Go about (to), virár de bórdo.
Good plier, bolinéro.
Good sailer, búque marinéro.
Goose-hook, gáncho de botavára.
Goose-wings, alétas de úna manguéra, calzónes.
Gore (cross), áspa,
Gore, brúsca.

Gore (total amount of), brúsca totál.
Goring-cloth, cuchíllo, páño de brúsca, luchíllo.
Gouge-channel, gubiadúra.
Grappling, rezón.
Grappling-iron or Grapnel, arpéo, anclóte, gáncho.
Grapplings (to warp with), espiár con rezónes.
Grating, ajedréz ó jaréta.
Gratings of the head, enjaretádo de próa.
Grave (to), despalmár, limpiár un búque.
Graving-dock, díque séco ó de construcción.
Great ensign, bandéra de gála.
Gripe of an anchor, tenedór de áncla.
Gripes, obénques ó bózas de láncha.
Grommet, aníllo ó roñáda.
Grommets of the eye-holes, roñádas de los solládos.
Ground, fóndo.
Ground (to), barár, tocár fóndo.
Groundage, derécho de puérto.
Ground-tackle, amarrazón de áncla.
Gudgeons or Googings, hémbras del timón.
Guest-rope, guía de fálsa amárra.
Gunports, portas.
Gunport-bars, bárras de portería.
Gun-room, sánta bárbara.
Gun-tackle, palanquín de cañón.
Gunwale, bórda, regála de la bórda del cómbes.
Guy, retenído.
Gybe (to), trasluchár.

H

Hail (to hail a ship), venír á voz.
Hale (to), halár.
Half-hitch, cóte.

Halliard or Halyard, dríza.
Hammock, cói, zafarráncho,
Hammock-cloth, empavesáda.
Hammock crowfoot, bolína de hamáca.
Hammock-sail, batayóla.
Handlead, sondalésa de máno.
Hand-over-hand, máno sobre máno.
Handsails, vélas manuáles.
Handspike, espéque.
Hang (to hang the rudder), montár el timón.
Hanging, arrúfo.
Hanging compass, agúja de cámara.
Hanging knees, cúrvas de álto abájo.
Hank, garrúcho de madéra, gáncho.
Hard-a-lee, orzár á la bánda.
Hard-a-weather, arribár á la bánda
Harpings, redóndos de la próa.
Harpoon, arpón.
Hatch or Hatchway, cuartél, escotílla.
Hatch-bars, bárras de las escotíllas.
Hat-money, cápa, sombréro.
Hatchway (fore), escotílla de próa.
Hatchway (magazine or after), escotílla de pópa.
Hatchway (main), escotílla mayór.
Haul (to), halár.
Haul (to haul aft the sheets), cazár las escótas.
Haul (to haul down the colors), arriár la bandéra.
Haul (to haul in), ronzár.
Haul (to haul off), zafárse.
Haul (to haul up), afirmár.
Haul (to haul up the courses in the brails), cargár
    los mayóres sobre las candelízas.
Haul the tack aboard, amurár.
Haul home (to), cazár, atracár.
Haul the wind (to), ceñír el viénto, abarloár.

Hauled (taut), téso.
Hauling-line, guía.
Haven, puérto.
Hawse-hole, escobén.
Hawse pieces, apóstoles.
Hawses, escobénes.
Hawse-pipes, canáles de plómo en los escobénes.
Hawse-plugs, tácos de los escobénes.
Hawser-laid rope, béta, guindaléza.
Head, galópe, gratíl, próa, cabéza del búque, púño
    de la péna.
Head (ahead), por la próa, á próa.
Head-cloth, paño del gratíl.
Head-fasts, amárras de próa.
Head-line or Head-rope, relínga del gratíl, varón.
Head-sea, mar de próa.
Head-sails, vélas delantéras ó de próa, aparéjo de próa.
Head-tabling, vaína del gratíl.
Headway, salída.
Headway (the), el andár, la arrancáda.
Head-wind, viénto por la próa.
Head of water, colúmna verticál de água.
Head-top, cabéza.
Head of stem, caperól.
Head of a mast, calcés.
Head (cathead), servióla.
Head (knee of the head), tajamár.
Heart, cuadernál ciégo.
Heave (to heave to), facheár, izár.
Heave down (to), arriár.
Heave (to), birár.
Heave (to heave ahead), birár para próa.
Heave (to heave the lead), hechár la sónda.
Heaver, alzapríma.
Heaving-in stays, viénto á fil de róda.

Heaving mallet, mázo.
Heavy sailer, búque pesádo.
Heel of a mast, talón, cóz ó pié de pálo.
Heel (to), escorár, inclinárse, tumbár sobre una bánda.
Height of the foot-gore, flécha de alunamiénto.
Height of the round, flécha de la cóla de páto.
Height between decks, altúra de entrepuéntes.
Helm, timón.
Helm (after-piece of the), azafrán del timón.
Helm (main-piece of the), mádre del timón.
Helm (to hang the), calár el timón.
Helm (the shift of the), cambiár el timón.
Helm (play of the), juégo del timón.
Helm's-man, timonél, timonéro.
Helm-port, liméra del timón.
Hemp, cáñamo, estópa.
High seas, álta mar.
Hindermost timber in the stern, almogáma.
Hitch, núdo, vuélta de cábo
Hitch (marling), trincafía.
Hog, escóba.
Hog (to hog a vessel), barrér un búque.
Hoist (the), caída, guínda.
Hoist (to), izár.
Hoist (to hoist home, to hoist atrip), reclamár.
Hoist in the middle, caída al céntro.
Hoist of a flag, vaína de bandéra.
Hold (the), bodéga.
Hold (depth of), puntál.
Hold (after), bodéga de pópa.
Hold (fore), bodéga de próa.
Hold (to trim the), abarrotár.
Hold water (to), ciár.
Hole, ojéte, groéra.
Hole (eyelet), olláo.

Hole (lubber's), bóca de lóbo.
Hollow, flécha de alunamiénto.
Home (close home), á besár.
Hood, carróza, caperúza de pálo, cubichéte.
Hood of the pump, tápa de la bómba.
Hook, garrúcho de madéra, gáncho.
Hook (thimble), gáncho con guardacábo.
Hook (tackle), gáncho de aparéjo.
Hook (cat), gáncho de la gáta.
Hook (swivel), gáncho giratório.
Hook (sail), gáncho de veléro.
Hook (goose), gáncho de botavára.
Hook (boat), bichéro.
Hook (to hook the cat to the anchor), enganchár la
     gáta al áncla.
Hooker, nómbre de una cláse de embarcación holandésa.
Hoop, súncho, árco.
Horns, quijádas.
Horse, marchapié, guardamancébo.
Horse of the bowsprit, guardamancébo del bauprés.
Horse of a yard, guardamancébo de una vérga.
Horse of a sail, nervío de una véla.
Horsing-iron, pitarása.
Hose (canvas), manguéra.
Hose (pump), ventiladór.
Hound, mésa, encapilladúra, cachólas.
Hounded, gratíl de vérga.
Hounds, encapilladúra.
House or Housing-line, pióla.
Housing of a mast, cabádo de un pálo.
Howker, úrca.
Hoy, nómbre de una embarcación de una véla.
Hulk or Hull, búque en rósca, cásco de un búque.
Hull (to hull a vessel), plantár un balázo en el cásco
     de un búque.
Hurricane, **uracán.**

I

Inclination of the compass, inclinación de la brújula.
Indraught, ábra, entráda.
Influx, inflújo, corriénte hácia tiérra.
Ingulf (to), engolfár, hechár á píque, perdérse entre tiérras.
Inlet, caléta, ábra.
Inner earing, empuñidúra de déntro.
Inner leech, caída de déntro.
Inning, terréno ganádo sobre la mar.
Invoice, factúra.
Iron-horse, batayóra.

J

Jack, bandéra de próa.
Jacksail (cross), mesána redónda.
Jackstaff, ásta de bandéra.
Jackstay, nérvio de una vérga.
Jaws, quijádas.
Jerk, gualdrapázo.
Jettison or jetson, cárga hecháda á la mar para la seguridád del búque.
Jetty-head, cabéza de muélle.
Jewel-blocks, motónes de las drízas de las rastréras.
Jib, fóque, maragúto.
Jib (parabolic), fóque parabólico.
Jib (standing), fóque principál, contrafóque.
Jib (middle), fofóque ó fóque segúndo.
Jib (concentrated or convergent), fóque de abánico ó fóque de cóncha.
Jib (first), fóque gránde.
Jib (second), fóque segúndo.

Jib (third), fóque tercéro.
Jib (storm), fóque de cápa.
Jib (chasing), fóque de cáza.
Jibboom, batallól, botalón de fóque.
Jib-halliard, dríza del fóque.
Jib-iron, arráca.
Jib-o'-jib, fóque volánte.
Jigger, aparejuélo, el palanquín de socaíre.
Jigger-tackle, lanteón, aparéjo de estríque.
Jollyboat, bóte (cuárto), botequín.
Junk, una embarcación chína, trózos de cáble viéjo.

K

Keckling, fórro de cáble.
Kedge, anclóte, una áncla pequéña.
Keel, quílla.
Keel (false), zapáta de quílla.
Keel (rabbit of the), alefríz de quílla.
Keel (scarfs of the), júntas de quílla.
Keel (sheathing of the), embón de quílla.
Keelage, deréchos de quílla.
Keelhale (to), pasár por la quílla.
Keel-rope, cábo imbornaléro de las varéngas.
Keelson or Kelson, sobrequílla.
Keep the sails full, andár en buénas vélas.
Keep away (to), amollár.
Keep (to keep the land aboard), mantenérse á vísta
      de la tiérra.
Keep (to keep the sea), estár á lárgo.
Kentledge, lingótes de fiérro que sirvén de lástre
      para movér un búque de un púnto á ótro.
Ketch, quéche; una embarcación de dos pálos.
Knee of iron, cúrva de hiérro.

Knee of the head, tajamár, cúrva capuchína, espolón.
Knee (upper part ot the), brázo superiór de la cúrva.
Knees (hanging), cúrvas de perálto ó de abájo.
Knees (lodging), cúrvas valónas.
Knees (helmport), cúrvas de contrayúgo.
Knees (wing-transom), cúrvas del yúgo principál.
Knees (deck-transom), cúrvas de la cubiérta.
Knees (small), curvatónes.
Knighthead, tragánte esteriór del bauprés.
Knighthead of the windlass, cépos ó bítas del molinéte.
Knightheads of the gears, guindástes.
Knittle, sardinéta.
Knot, núdo, mílla, señál de la corredéra.
Knot (wall), píña.
Knuckle-timbers, alétas de las serviólas.

L

Labor (to), trabajár en mar gruésa.
Labor (a ship that labors much), un búque que balancéa múcho.
Laborsome ship, búque tòrmentóso.
Lace (to), aculebrár, cosér.
Lace in (to), embasár.
Lacing-line, pasadéra.
Laden ship, búque cargádo.
Lanch, láncha.
Landfall, recaláda.
Lantern (top), fárol de la cófa.
Lanyard or Laniard, acolladór, sardinéla.
Lanyards of the shrouds, acolladóres de los obénques.
Lanyards of the stoppers, mogélles de las hózas.
Lanyards of the buoy, rebénques de cabéza de la bóya.
Larboard, babór.

Large, á un lárgo.

Large (to sail), navegár con viénto lárgo.

Lash (to), abarbetár, amarrár, ligár, trincár, falcaceár.

Lash (to lash with twisting), atortorár.

Lash up (to), cerrár.

Lashing (the), amarradúra.

Lashing, tortór, ligadúra, barbéta.

Lashings of the longboat, obénques de la láncha.

Lashing rings, argóllas de amárra.

Latchings, embasadúra.

Lateen boat (a small), laúd.

Lateen-brace, orzapópa.

Lateen-braces, davántes.

Lateen-halliard, dríza de enténa.

Lateen-masthead, capcés.

Lateen-rig, aparéjo latíno.

Lateen-rigged vessel, búque latíno.

Lateen-sail (storm), píchola.

Lateen-sail (flamish eye), maníla.

Lateen-sail, latína ó véla de búrro.

Lateen-yard, enténa.

Launch (to), botár, ó échar una embarcación al água.

Lay-days, días de demóra ó estadías.

Lay-days (over) or demurrage, sobreestadías ó días de demóra.

Lay (to lay ropes), colchár cábos.

Lay (to lay alongside), abarloár, atracár.

Lay on her sides (to), dormírse.

Lead (hand), sondalésa ó escandállo de máno.

Lead (deep-sea), escandállo mayór.

Lead (to heave the), hechár la sónda.

Leak (to), hacér água.

Leak (to spring a), abrírse una entráda al água.

Ledges of the gratings, barrótes de los enjaretádos.

Lee, sotavénto.

Lee-arm, péna.

Lee-bowline, bolína de revés.

Lee-braces, brázos de sotavénto.

Lee-shore, costa de sotavénto.

Lee-side, lúa ó bánda de sotavénto.

Leeward (to), á sotavénto.

Leeward (under the), á sotavénto.

Leeward ship (a), búque rancéro ó sotaventeadór.

Leeward (to fall to), abatír.

Leeway, abatimiénto ó derríba.

Leech, cuchíllo, caída.

Leech or After-leech, valúma.

Leech-cloth, páño de cuchíllo.

Leech-gore, brúsca de cuchíllo.

Leech-linings, sobresános.

Leech-rope, relínga de caída ó relínga de la valúma.

Leech-line, apagapenól.

Leech-tabling, vaína de la valúma.

Left-handed, de la mála máno.

Length, eslóra, lárgo.

Length of a ship, eslóra de un búque.

Length of a yard, cruzámen.

Lessen (to), amortiguár.

Let go (to), largár.

Let go a-main (to), arriár en bánda.

Let go quickly (to), largár en bánda.

Let out (to), largár.

Letter of marque, paténte de corso.

Level line, línea de água.

Lie to (to), atravesárse, capeár ó estár á la cápa.

Lie on (to), estár en cárga.

Lie by (to), atravesárse, facheár.

Lie alongside (to), dár á la bánda.

Lie under the sea (to), capeár.

Lift, amantíllo.

Lifts (topping-lifts), amantíllos de botavára.
Lifts (handing-lifts), mostáchos.
Lifting-jacks, prénsas bidraulícas de máno.
Light airs, ventolínas.
Light canvas, brinéte.
Light winds, ventolínas.
Light (to), aligerár, hacér mas boyánte.
Lighter or Barge, lanchón, gavárra, chalána.
Lighter (ballast), lanchón de lastrár.
Lighterage, gabarráje.
Lighterman, lanchonéro.
Lighthouse, fáro, fanál, lúz.
Limber-holes, imbornáles de las varéngas.
Limber-rope, cábo imbornaléro de las varéngas.
Line-of-battle ship, navío de álto bórdo.
Line, béta, cábo, vaivén.
Line (untarred), béta blánca.
Line (tarred), béta négra, alquitranáda.
Line (head), relínga del gratíl, varón.
Line (rattling), baibén, vaivén.
Line (strengthening), batidór, nérvio de la véla latína.
Line (rhumb), rúmbo.
Line (spilling), apagavéla.
Line (house), pióla.
Line (triving), perigállo.
Line (lacing), pasadéra.
Line (to), remendár.
Line (marling or marline), merlín.
Line (lead), sondalésa.
Line (furling), lanteón.
Line (ram), liénza.
Line (marking), liénza.
Line (water), línea de água.
Line (load-water), línea de cárga.
Line (level) línea de água.

Line (log), corredéra.
Lines (leech), apagapenólcs.
Lines (furling), tomadórcs.
Lines (spilling), trápas.
Lining, remiéndo.
Lining (top), batidéro.
Lining canvas, lóna de refuérzo.
Linings, refuérzos.
Linings (leech), sobresános.
Little boat, barquílla.
Locker, cajón ó alacéna de cámara.
Locker (shot), chilléra.
Lodging-knees, cúrvas valónas.
Log, corredéra y carretél, el ló.
Log-board, tabléta de bitácora.
Log-line, corredéra.
Log-book, cuadérno de bitácora, diário de navegación.
Log-reel, carretél.
Loof, lóf.
Loof-framc, cuadérna de lóf.
Loof (to), ceñír cl viénto, ír de ló ó lóf.
Look-out (the), vigía.
Loom of an oar, guión.
Loom-gale, fugáda bonancíble.
Look-out, tópe.
Longboat, bóte láncha, bárca mayór, falúa.
Long-work, púnto de váina, púnto de telár.
Loop, gáza.
Loophole, tronéra.
Loosen (to loosen a sail), largár una véla.
Low-reefs, rízos chícos.
Lower (to), tiramollár, arriár.
Lower end of a lateen yard, cár.
Lower sails, vélas bájas.
Lower-studdingsail-boom, tangón.

Lubber's hole, bóca de lóbo.
Luff, amúra, gratíl.
Luff (to), ceñír el viénto.
Luff (to keep the), orzár tódo.
Luff (to luff round), metér todo á lof.
Luff (to luff up), tomár por avánte.
Luff (to spring the), partír el púño.
Luff-tackle, aparéjo de bolineár.
Lug (to), halár, tirár los cábos.
Lugger, lúgre, embarcación pesáda con véla cuadráda.
Lugger (Biscayan), trincadúra.
Lugsail, véla mistica, véla tarquína, véla al tércio.
Lying-to, estár á la cápa.

M

Mademast, pálo de piézas, compuésto.
Magazine, pañól de pólvora, sánta bárbara.
Main and topsails, aparéjo principál.
Main and fore-trysail, cangréjos.
Main-boom, botavára.
Main-boom (throat of the), bóca de botavára.
Main-brace, bráza de la mayór.
Main-braces, brázos mayóres.
Main-breadth, mánga, el firme.
Main-course, mayór redónda.
Main-deck, cubiérta principál.
Main-gears, dríza de la mayór.
Main-hatchway, escotílla mayór.
Mainland, continénte.
Main-mast, pálo mayór.
Main-rigging, járcia mayór.
Main-royalmast, masteléro de sobrejuanéte mayór.
Main-royalyard, vérga de sobrejuanéte mayór.

Main-sail, cangréjo mayór, mayór.
Main-sail (storm), mayór de cápa, quechemarina.
Main-sheet, escóta de la mayór.
Main-staysail, véla de estái mayór, carbonéra.
Maintop, cófa mayór, ó de gávia.
Maintop-braces, brázos de gávia.
Main-topgallant-braces, brázos de juanéte mayór.
Main-topgallant-sail, véla de juanéte mayór.
Main-topgallant-staysail, véla de estái de juanéte mayór
Main-topgallant-royal, véla de sobrejuanéte mayór.
Main-topgallant-mast, masteléro de juanéte mayór.
Main-topgallantyard, vérga de juanéte mayór.
Main-topgallant-royalyard, vérga de sobrejuanéte
    mayór.
Main-topmast, masteléro de gávia, mayór.
Main-topmast-staysail, véla de estái de gávia.
Main-topsail, gávia.
Main-topsail schooner, goléta de gávias.
Main-topsail-halliard, dríza de gávia.
Main-topsailyard, vérga de gávia.
Main-topyard, verga de gávia.
Mainwhale, cínta mayór, cínta de la mánga.
Mainyard, vérga mayór.
Make (to make sail), largár véla.
Make (to make sternway), hacér camíno para pópa.
Make (to make headway), hacér camíno, andár.
Make (to make the land), navegár hácia la tiérra,
    tomár la tiérra.
Mallet, macéta, mázo.
Mallet (caulking), macéta de calafáte.
Mallet (driving), macéta de ajustár.
Mallet (heaving), mázo, macéta.
Mallet (serving), macéta de aferrár.
Man (to), armár, tripulár.
Man a boat (to), esquifár un bóte.

Man the capstan (to), guarnír el cabrestánte.
Manger, cája de água.
Man-of-war, navío, búque de guérra.
Man-rope, guardamancébo.
Manœuvre (to), maniobrár.
Marine, marína.
Maritime, maríno.
Mark, piquéte.
Marl (to), trincafiár, empalomár.
Marline or Marling-line, merlín.
Marling-hitch, trincafia.
Marling-spike, pasadór.
Marque (letter of), paténte de córso.
Mask (to mask a ship), disfrazár la bandéra.
Mast, masteléro, pálo.
Mast (sprung), pálo rendído.
Mast (fished), pálo reforzádo.
Mast (fore), pálo de trinquéte.
Mast (fore-royal), masteléro de sobrejuanéte de próa.
Mast (fore-top), masteléro de velácho ó de próa.
Mast (fore-topgallant), masteléro de juanéte de próa.
Mast (made), pálo de piézas, compuésto.
Mast (main), pálo mayór.
Mast (main-royal), masteléro de sobrejuanéte mayór.
Mast (main-top), masteléro de gávia, ó mayór.
Mast (main-topgallant), masteléro de juanéte mayór.
Mast (mizen), pálo de mesána.
Mast (mizen-top), masteléro de sobremesána.
Mast (mizen-topgallant), masteléro de juanéte de sobremesána.
Mast (mizen-royal), masteléro de sobreperiquíto.
Mast (pole), pálo mácho, pálo típle, pálo enterízo, pálo de una piéza.
Mast (single), masteléro enterízo.
Mast (spare), masteléro de respéto.

Mast (top), masteléro.
Mast (to), arbolár.
Mast (to spend a), perdér un pálo.
Mast (to), arbolár un pálo.
Mast-gore, brúsca de la caída de próa.
Mast-head, calcés.
Mast-rope, relónga del pálo.
Masts (lower or standing-masts), pálos principáles.
Masting, arboladúra.
Master a sail (to), cerrár una véla.
Master, patrón, capitán, maéstre.
Mat, pálléte ó palléta.
Mat (chafed), palléta afelpáda.
Mate, pilóto.
Mate (boatswain's), guardián del contramaéstre.
Mate (master's), contramaéstre.
Mate (steward's), ayudánte del despenséro.
Matriculation, matrícula.
Maul, macéta, mázo.
Measure (to), arqueár.
Measure down (to), palmeár.
Measurement-bill, certificádo de toneláje.
Merchant flag, bandéra mercánte.
Merchantman, búque mercánte.
Mess, comída, una partída de la compánia de un búque que cóme júnta.
Mess (steward of the), ranchéro.
Messenger, aparéjo para llevár el áncla.
Messenger (to clap a messenger on the cable), cosér un aparéjo al cáble.
Middle-band, fája de médio.
Middle-deck, segúnda cubiérta.
Middle-jib, fofóque, fóque segúndo.
Middle-staysail, véla de estái volánte.
Midship-beam báo maéstro.

Midship-bend or frame, cuadérna maéstra.
Midshipman, guárdia marína.
Mile, mílla náutica ó núdo.
Miss (to), mancár.
Miss (to miss stays), faltár la viráda.
Mizen or Mizzen, mesána, batículo.
Mizen (to balance the), tomár rízos en la mesána.
Mizen-boom, cáza escóta, botavára.
Mizen-mast, pálo de mesána.
Mizen-royal, sobreperiquíto.
Mizen-royalyard, vérga de sobreperiquíto.
Mizen-royalmast, masteléro de sobreperiquíto.
Mizen-shrouds, járcia de mesána.
Mizen-staysail, véla de estái de mesána, matasoldádos.
Mizen-topgallant-staysail, véla de estái de periquíto.
Mizen-topgallantsail, juanéte de sobremesána.
Mizen-topsailyard, vérga de sobremesána.
Mizen-topgallantyard, vérga de juanéte de sobremesána
Mizen-topgallantmast, masteléro de juanéte de sobre-
    mesána.
Mizen-topmast, masteléro de sobremesána.
Mizen-topsail, sobremesána.
Mizen-topmast-staysail, véla de estái de sobremesána.
Mizen-trysail, mesána de cápa.
Moor (to), amarrár, atár con áncla, situárse.
Moor (to moor by the stern), amarrár con una reguéra,
    amarrár el búque de pópa.
Moor (to moor by the head), amarrár con las amárras
    de próa.
Moor (to moor with a spring), amarrár con codéra
    sobre el cáble.
Moorings, amárras fíjas.
Mooring-rings, argóllas de amarrár.
Mooring-swivels, ramáles de cadéna.
Moor's-head, tamboréte.

Mooter, él que trabája los tolétes.
Mortise, escopleadúra, ramúra, cagéra.
Mould, grúa de táblas, plantílla.
Mouse, barriléte.
Mouse (to mouse a hook), amarrár un gáncho.
Muster-roll, ról de la tripulación.
Mulet, muléta.

N

Nails, clávos.
Nails (clasp), clávos de ála de mósca.
Nails (clinker), clávos de tinglár.
Nails (sheathing), clávos de entablár.
National flag, bandéra de guérra.
Naval tactitian, maniobrísta.
Nave-line, perigállo, de racaménto.
Navigate (to), navegár.
Navy, marína.
Neap, bájo, menguánte.
Neap-tide, maréa bája.
Neck or Nock, púño de la bóca, empuñidúra de la bóca.
Neck-laces (chain), súncho de las arraigádas.
Needle (sail), agúja, capotéra.
Needle (bolt-rope), agúja de relínga.
Nettings, enjaretádos.
Nettings (quarter), rédes de combáte.
Nippers, mojélas.
Northing, la diferencía de latitúd que hace un búque
     en su rúmbo.
Notch, ranúra.
Nut of an anchor, oréja de áncla.

O

Oakum, estópa para calafateár.

Oar, rémo.

Oar (flat of an), pála de rémo.

Oars (to ship the), armár los rémos.

Oars (hold on your), álza los rémos.

Off (to be off a port), estár á la altúra de un puérto.

Offing (to stand for the), corrér al lárgo.

Offward, al lárgo de la cósta.

Open, abiérto.

Orlop, solládo, cubiérto del solládo.

Orlop-beam, báo del solládo, báo vacío.

Orthodromicks or Orthodromy, orthodromía, navega-
    ción en linéa récta.

Out of trim, mál estivádo,

Out (all sails), aparéjo lárgo.

Out-bound ship, búque de travesía.

Outer-earing, empuñidúra de fuéra.

Outer-leech, caída de fuéra.

Outfit, lo necesarío para equipár un búque.

Outrigger, botavára, horquéta, pescántc de bánda
    para carenár, púntal de tópe, cuérnos de la
    crucéta.

Outriggers of the top, pescántes de las cófas, ó cuérnos
    de las cófas.

Out-sail (to), pasár á otro búque navegándo.

Outward bound, en viáge de salída.

Overhaul (to), tiramollár, registrár, recorrér.

Over-masted ship, búque de múcha guínda.

Overset (to), zozobrár.

Overboard, á la már.

Overboard (to throw), echár á la már.

Owner, naviéro, armadór.

P

Packet, paquebóte.
Painter, amárra del bóte, amárra de la láncha.
Palendar, un embarcación ahora en desúso.
Palm, rempújo.
Palm-thimble, dádo.
Parabolic-jib, fóque parabólico.
Parcel (to), aforrár las costúras.
Parcelling, precínta, cápa.
Parliament-heel, pandóles.
Parrel or Parral, racaménto.
Parrel (ribs of the), liébres del racaménto.
Parrel-trucks, vertéllos del racaménto.
Parrel-rope, bastárdo de recaménto.
Part (running), guárne.
Partners of the capstan, mallétes del cabrestánte.
Partners of the mainmast, fogonadúras del pálo mayór.
Partners, fogonadúra, mallétes.
Partner's-rim, golílla.
Passarado or l'assaree, bardágo.
Patache, patáche.
Paunch, palléte.
Pavilion, pabéllon, bandéra.
Pawl of the capstan, lingüéte del cabrestánte.
Pawl (supporter of the), descánso del lingüéte.
Pawls (hanging), lingüétes de por álto.
Pay (to pay a ship's bottom), embreár el fóndo de
    un búque.
Pay (to pay out a cable), largár ó arriár un cáble.
Peak, púño del píco, péna, peñol.
Peak-earing, empuñidúra del píco.
Peak-halliards, drízas de la péna.
Peek, peñól.
Peek up (to), embicár.

Peeked, embicadúra.
Pegging-awl, punzón.
Pendant, coróna, gallardéte.
Pendant (broad), rábo de gállo, gallardetón, cornéta.
Pendant (fish), amánte.
Pennants, amántes.
Petty-tally, ración para la tripulación.
Pier, muélle.
Pillow of the bowsprit, descánso del bowprés.
Pillows of the mast-heads, almohádas de las járcias.
Pilots' boat, pailebót.
Pilot (coast), pilóto de cósta.
Pilot (sea), pilóto de altúra.
Pilotage, pilotáge.
Pilotage (book of), derrotéro.
Pilotage (rates of), timonáge.
Pin, clavíja.
Pin of a boat, toléte.
Pin of a block, pérno de roldána, pérno de motón.
Pin-rack, cabilléro.
Pink, pingüe, una embarcación.
Pinksterned, estrécho á la pópa.
Pinnace, primér bóte, pináza, una embarcación de
     rémo y véla.
Pins (belaying), cavíllas.
Pitch, bréa, péz.
Pitch (to), arfár.
Pitchbrush, escopéro.
Pitching-ship, cabeceadór.
Pitching of a vessel, cabezáda de un búque.
Plait (to), señalár.
Plank (the planks of a ship), tablage, tablazón.
Plank (to plank the deck), entablár la cubiérta.
Plat, badérna.
Plates (backstay), cadénas de los brandáles.

Plunge (to), cabeceár.
Ply (to ply to windward), barloventeár.
Plying (the), el hacér camíno contra el viénto.
Point of the compass, rúmbo.
Points, rízos.
Pointed rope or Pointing, rábo de ráta.
Pole, galópe.
Poleacre, polácra, una embarcación en úso en el Levánte
Poleacre-settee, velachéro.
Pole-mast, pálo típle, enterízo, de una piéza.
Poles (under bare poles), á pálo séco, á la bretóna.
Pontoon, cháta.
Poop, pópa, toldílla, tóldo de pópa.
Poop (to), encajárse por la pópa.
Poop-decked ship, búque de toldílla.
Poop-royal, chopéta.
Port, babór.
Port (bar), puérto con bárra.
Port (close), puérto cerrádo.
Port (free), puérto fránco, líbre de deréchos.
Port (hard-a-port), á babór tódo.
Port (helm), liméra.
Port (light), ventaníllas.
Port (to), á, por, de babór.
Port (to touch at a), hacér escála.
Port (the ship heels to port), el búque cáe sobre el babór.
Port-cells, batipórtes.
Portlast (to ride a), estár con los masteléros arriádos.
Port-lids, tapadéros de las pórtas.
Port-ropes, amántes de pórtas.
Port-sails, vélas de alastrár.
Port-tackles, aparejuélos de pórtas.
Ports (ballast), pórtas de alastrár.
Ports (raft), pórtas de recíbo.
Powder-room, sánta bárbara, pañól de pólvora.

Practic or Practique, práctica.
Prame, un bárco cháto.
Preventer, volánte.
Preventer-backstays, contrabrandáles.
Preventer-brace, contrabráza.
Preventer-lifts, contraamantíllos.
Preventer-plates, estríbos de las cadénas.
Preventer-shrouds, contraobénques.
Preventer-sheets, contraescótas.
Preventer-stay, contraestái, estái folár.
Preventer-tacks, contraamúras.
Prick (to prick the sails), recosér las vélas.
Prick (to prick the chart), marcár sobre la cárta el
        camíno del búque.
Pricker, punzón.
Privateer, corsário.
Props of the cut-water, escóras del tajamár.
Prow, flécha, próa, espolón de tabéque.
Puckering, salomónicos.
Puddening, guirnálda.
Puddening of a mast, guirnálda de pálo.
Puddening of an anchor, anetúra.
Pull (to), bogár.
Pull (to pull ahead), tirár, avánte,
Pulley, poléa, roldána.
Pulley-piece, armadúra de bárca.
Pump, bómba, tragánte.
Pump (chain), bómba de cadéna.
Pump (to fetch the), cargár la bómba.
Pump (to man the), armár la bómba.
Pump-box, mortéro de bómba.
Pump-brake, guimbaléte.
Pump-chamber, almacén de bómbas.
Pump-dale, adála, dála.
Pump-hook, sacanábo.

Pump-hose, manguéra.
Pump-nails, tachuélas de bómba.
Pump-ram, ariéte de una bómba.
Pump-spear, ásta de bómba.
Pump-ship, la bómba.
Pump-well, cája de bómbas.
Punch, punzón.
Punts, plánchas de água.
Purser, contadór, maéstre de víveres.
Pursue (to), cazár.
Push (to push off), desatracár.
Put in (to), entrár en un puérto.
Put to sea (to), salír á la már.
Putty, macílla.

Q

Quarantain or Quarantine, cuarenténa.
Quarter, á un lárgo.
Quarter (the) ánca, cuadra de pópa.
Quarter-clothes, empavesádas.
Quarter-deck, alcazár.
Quarter-deck awning, tóldo del alcazár.
Quarter-gallery, jardín.
Quarter-gunners, artilléros de marína.
Quarter-gaskets, tomadóres del tércio.
Quarter-netting, rédes de combáte.
Quarter-pieces, montántes,
Quarter-point of the compass, cuárto de la brújula.
Quarter-rails, batayólas.
Quarter-watch, guárdia.
Quarter-wind, viénto por ánca.
Quay, muélle.
Quick-work, óbra víva.

R

Rabbet or Rabbit, alefríz.
Rack, liébre.
Rag (to), rozár.
Ragbolt, pérno harponádo.
Rail for the belaying-pins, cabilléro.
Rail (hammock), batayóla.
Rails (head), pérchas.
Rails (rough-tree), barándas,
Rails (waist), varéngas.
Rake, caído de pálo.
Rake of stem, lanzamiénto.
Ram-line, liénza.
Range of belaying-pins, cabilléro.
Range of a cable, adúja de cáble.
Ranges, cornamúsas.
Rapid current of sea water, aguáge.
Rapidity, salída.
Ratchet-braces, lingüétes.
Ratchet-wheel, ruéda de lingüétes.
Rate, porte.
Rate of sailíng, camíno.
Ratlines or Rattlings, rebénques, flechástes, aflecháten
Rattling-line, baibén, vaivén.
Rattlings, flechadúra.
Raven's duck, lonéta.
Ream (to), calafateár.
Reckoning, estíma.
Reckoning (dead), rúmbo estimádo.
Reef, rízo.
Reef-band, fája de rízos.
Reef-cringle, púños de las pájas.
Reef-earing, empuñidúra de los rízos.
Reef-line, cábo de tomár rízos.

Reef-tackle, amánte de rízos.

Reef-tackles, aparejuélos de rízos, palanquínes de rízos

Reef-tackle pieces, refuérzos de los amántes de rízos.

Reef-tackle-cringle, garrúcho del amánte de rízos.

Reef of a log, carretél.

Reef (bag), rízos chícos.

Reef (balance), antagálla.

Reef (close), rízos chícos, última fája.

Reef (low), rízos chícos, última fája.

Reef (to), arrizár, tomár un rízo.

Reef (to let out a), largár un rízo.

Reef (to be close-reefed), con todos los rízos tomádos, navegár arrizádo.

Reefs, andána de rízos.

Reefs (to shake the), largár rízos.

Reeming-mallet, macéta de calafáte.

Reeve (to), cosér, pasár, guarnír.

Reeving, cosidúra.

Refit, ponér un búque en buén estádo para navegár.

Register, matrícula.

Rend, costúra de los tablónes.

Revenue vessel, guardacóstas.

Reversed gore, brúsca de revés.

Reversed goring-cloths, contracuchíllos.

Rhumb-line, rúmbo.

Ribs of a ship, ligazónes de un búque.

Ribs of a parrel, liébres de recaménto.

Ride (to ride at anchor), estár fondeádo.

Ride (riding at anchor in this port), súrto en este puérto.

Riders, sobreplánes, costíllas interióres.

Riders (floor), sobreplánes del fóndo.

Riders (after-floor), sobreplánes popéses del fóndo.

Riders (lower-futtock), genóles de sobreplánes.

Riders (second-futtock), ligazónes de sobreplánes.

Ride-ropes of the head-netting, nérvios de las rédes de próa.

Ridge-rope, relónga de cúmbre.
Riding hard, tormentóso al áncla.
Riding easy, descansádo al áncla.
Rig (to), aparejár.
Rig (lateen), aparéjo latíno.
Rig (to rig a sail), guarnír una véla.
Rigged (square), aparéjo redóndo, aparéjo de crúz.
Rigger, aparejadór.
Rigging, manióbra, aparéjo, guarniménto.
Rigging (standing), manióbra fírme, járcia muérta.
Rigging (running), manióbra volánte, járcia de labór.
Rigging (rope), járcia.
Rigging (main), járcia mayór.
Right (to), adrizár.
Right-handed, de la buéna máno.
Rim up (to), encojér.
Rim (partner's), golílla.
Ring, argáneo, biróla con chavéta.
Ring-bolt, cáncamo, argólla.
Ring-tailsail, maricangállo.
Ring-tail, candónga.
Rise, arrúfo.
Rising (the), astílla muérta.
Rising (the dead), astílla muérta.
Roach (to), alunár.
Roaching (the), alunamiénto.
Roach-leech, curvedád.
Robbings or Robands, envérgues.
Rollers, polínes, rollétes.
Rolling, balánce.
Rolling-tackle, aparéjo de rolín.
Room, pañól.
Room (sail), pañól de vélas.
Rope, cábo, béta, járcia, cuérda.
Rope (after-leech), relónga de la caída de pópa.

Rope-band, envérgue.
Rope (buoy), orínque.
Rope (bolt), relínga.
Rope (cluc), relónga del púño.
Rope (entering), guardamancébo del portalón.
Rope (foot), relónga del pujámen.
Rope (fore-leech), relónga de la caida de próa.
Rope (guest), guía de fálsa amárra.
Rope (head), relínga del gratíl.
Rope (hawser-laid), béta, guindaléza.
Rope (leech), relónga de caída, relónga de valúma.
Rope (mast), relónga del pálo.
Rope (man), guardamancébo.
Rope (pointed), rábo de rúta.
Rope (parrel), bastárdo de racaménto.
Rope (ridge), relónga de cúmbre.
Rope a sail (to), relingár.
Rope (top), viradór, amánte viradór.
Rope (tho standing part of a), arraigádo.
Rope (whitc), béta blánca.
Ropes (awning side), nérvio de tóldo.
Ropes (wheel), guardínes.
Ropes (tiller), guardínes.
Rope's-end, chicóte de cábo.
Rope-rigging, járcia.
Ropeyard, cordelería.
Ropeyarn, filástica.
Ropewalk, cordelería.
Roughtree, pércha de arboladúra.
Roughtree-nails, posavérgas.
Round (to go), virár.
Round quarter, pópa redónda.
Round-stitch, púnto de bigorílla.
Round-stern ship, cúlo de móna.
Round-seam, bigorílla.

Round in (to), halár en redondo.
Round up the beams (to), volvér para arriba los báos.
Rounding, fórro de cáble.
Rounding of the foot, cóla de páto.
Rouse (to), zallár, halár un cáble, arronzár un cáble.
Row (to), bogár.
Rowlocks, chamucéras.
Royal, juanéte.
Royal (mizen), sobreperiquíto.
Royal (main-royalyard), vérga de sobrejuanéte mayór.
Royal (fore-royalyard), vérga de sobrejuanéte de próa.
Royal (mizen-royalyard), vérga de sobreperiquíto.
Royal-standard, estandárte réal.
Royals, sobrejuanétes.
Rub (to rub down), planchár.
Rubber, mordáza.
Rubbing-paunch, gimélga.
Rudder, timón.
Rudder-hole, liméra.
Rudder-pintles, máchos del timón.
Run (to), laboreár.
Run, racél.
Run into port (to), entrár un puérto.
Run close-hauled (to), corrér a bolína haláda.
Run out a warp (to), tendér una espía.
Rungs, varéngas plánes.
Rungheads, escóas.
Runner and tackle, aparéjo de amánte y estrélla.
Runners, avántes.
Runner of a tackle, amánte de aparéjo.
Runner of a crowfoot, perigállo de aráña.
Running, tíra, laboréo.
Running ropes or Running rigging, cábos de labór.
Running-part, guárne.
Russian duck, liénzo de Rúsia.

S

Saddle, arrúfo.
Sag to leeward (to), írse á la rónza.
Saick, saétia, embarcación Túrca.
Sail, véla.
Sail (a very sharp-angled lateen), véla espigáda.
Sail before the wind (to), navegár en pópa.
Sail by the wind (to), ceñír, navegár con viénto de través
Sail (boom-fore), trinquéte con botalón.
Sail (Bermudoe), áurica.
Sail (concentrated), véla de cóncha, véla de abaníco.
Sail (cross-jack), mesána redónda. ·
Sail close-hauled (to), navegár á bolína.
Sail clue (to), ceñír.
Sail (fore), trinquéte.
Sail (fore-and-aft), véla de cuchíllo.
Sail (fore-top), velácho.
Sail (fore-topgallant), juanéte de próa.
Sail (flying-topgallant), juanéte volánte.
Sail (gaff-topgallant), sóbre escandalósa.
Sail large (to), navegár en lárgo.
Sail (lug), véla mística, tarquína, véla al tércio.
Sail (lateen), véla latína.
Sail (main), mayór.
Sail (main-top), gávia.
Sail (main-topgallant), juanéte mayór.
Sail (main-topgallant-royal), sobrejuanéte mayór.
Sail (mizen), mesána.
Sail (mizen-topgallant), juanéte de sobremesána.
Sail (mizen-topsail), sobremesána.
Sail (plan of), pláno de velámen.
Sail (square), véla cuádra, redónda.
Sail (sprit), véla de abaníco, cebadéra.
Sail (scudding), tréo.

Sail (slack), véla faldóna.
Sail (smoke), guardahúma.
Sail (studding), ála, rastréra.
Sail (to flat in), acuartelár.
Sail (to), navegár.
Sail (to strike), arriár una véla.
Sail (try), véla de fortúna.
Sail (the furling of a), rifadúra.
Sail (topgallant), juanéte.
Sail (to set), largár véla, orientár.
Sail (to set a), ponérse á la véla, hacérse á la véla.
Sail (to rig a), guarnír.
Sail (to unfurl a), largár una véla.
Sail (trapezoid), véla de cuchíllo.
Sail (tabled), véla envaináda.
Sail (to sail along the coast), costeár.
Sail right before the wind (to), navegár á dos púños.
Sail with the wind on the beam (to), navegár con
     el viénto á través.
Sail with a scant wind (to), navegár con bolína.
Sail close-hauled (to), navegár ciñéndo el viénto.
Sail (unfinished sail without the tabling), véla en sáco.
Sail (water), rastréro.
Sail (wind), ventiladór, manguéra.
Sailcloth, liénzo, lóna.
Sail-cutting (practical), trazár practicaménte.
Sail-hook, gáncho de veléro.
Sail-loft, obradór de vélas, tingládo de vélas.
Sail-maker, maéstro veléro, maéstro de vélas.
Sail-making, construcción de vélas.
Sail-room, pañól de vélas.
Sailing free, navegár á un lárgo.
Sailing ship or vessel, búque de véla.
Sailing (the), el andár, hacér camíno.
Sailing-needle, agúja de capotéra.

Sails, velámen.
Sails (aft), vélas de pópa, aparéjo mayór.
Sails out (all), aparéjo lárgo.
Sails (flying), vélas menúdas.
Sails (fore-topmast-studding), álas de velácho.
Sails (head or fore), vélas de próa.
Sails (lower), vélas bájas.
Sails (main-topmast-studding), álas de gávia.
Sails (main-topgallant-studding),álas de juanéte mayór
Sails (set of), velámen, juégo de vélas.
Sails (to mend the), remendár las vélas.
Sails (upper), vélas áltas.
Sailor, marinéro.
Sailyard, vérga.
Salvage, salvácha.
Saucer, la parte que recíbe el espigón del cabrestánte.
Save-all, rastréro.
Save-all-topsail, gávia volánte.
Scarf (to), encabezár.
Scarfing, encabezadúra.
Scantlings, las grúas de táblas.
Schooner (a main-topsail), goléta de gávias.
Schooner (a topsail), goléta de velácho.
Schooner (brig-rigged forward), bergantín goléta.
Schooner (fore-and-aft), goléta.
Scoop, vertedór, achicadór.
Score, ranúra.
Score of a block for a strop, mortájas para las gázas de cábo.
Scrapers, rasquétas.
Scud (to), corrér.
Scud a hull (to), abrotonár.
Scud before the wind (to), corrér con viénto en pópa.
Scud before the sea (to), corrér con mar en pópa.
Scud under bare poles (to), corrér á pálo séco.

Scud with both sheets aft (to), corrér á dos púños.
Scuddingsail, tréo.
Sculler, bóte de un reméro.
Scuppers, imbornáles.
Scuttle, escotíllón.
Scuttles (cabin), lumbréras de camaróte.
Scuttles of the masts, fogonadúras.
Sea, la mar.
Sea anchor, áncla de mar.
Sea card, rósa nautíca.
Sea chart, cárta de mareár.
Sea voyage, campáña de mar.
Sea (heavy swell in the), mar de léva.
Sea runs high (the), la mar está muy crecída.
Sea (to put to), salír á la mar.
Seaboy, gruméte.
Seaman, marinéro, maríno.
Searoom, mar áncha.
Seam, costúra de los tablónes.
Seam (round), bigorílla.
Seams (broad), péjes.
Seams (to pay the), embreár las costúras.
Seat of a rower, bancáda.
Second jib, fóque segúndo.
Seel or Heel (to), tumbár.
Seeling, balánce de un búque.
Seize (to), abarbetár, amarrár, dar una ligadúra.
Seize with rushes (to), enjuncár.
Seizing (the), amarradúra, ligadúra.
Selvage, orílla, estróbos para los obénques y brandáles.
Send up (to), guindár.
Sennit, gajéta, trénza.
Serve (to), aforrár.
Serve a rope (to), aforrár un cábo.
Service, fórro de cáble.

Serving, guarnimiénto.
Serving board, paléta de forrár.
Serving mallet, macéta de aforrár.
Set aback (to), braceár en fácha.
Set athwart (to), atravesárse.
Set rings (to), engargolár.
Set sails (to), envelár.
Set up the shrouds (to), atesár las járcias.
Setbolt, botadór.
Settee, saétia, mística, un navío con dos pálos.
Setting fid, burél.
Shake (to), fameár, tocár.
Shallop, chalúpa.
Shank of the anchor, cáña del áncla.
Shankpainter, bóza de la uña del áncla.
Shape a course (to), ponérse en rúmbo.
Sharp-bottomed ship (a), búque de múchos delgádos.
Sheave, roldána.
Sheave-axletree, pérno de roldána.
Sheave-hole, cajéra.
Sheave-holes of the sheets, escotéras.
Sheepshank (to), hacér margaríta en un cábo.
Sheer, arúfa, arufadúra.
Sheer (a ship with a great), búque muy arrufádo.
Sheer off (to), alargárse.
Sheers, cabría de arbolár.
Sheerwale, arrúfo.
Sheet, escóta.
Sheet (to), cazár.
Sheet-anchor, áncla de esperánza.
Sheet cable, cáble mayór.
Sheet home (to), cazár á besár.
Sheet-hole, escótera.
Sheets aft (both), navegár en pópa.
Sheets (topsail), escotínes.

Sheets (to haul aft the), cazár las escótas.
Sheets (to haul home the topsail), cazár el escotín á besár
Sheets (to ease off the), dar un sálto á las escótas.
Sheets (to let fly the), arriár las escótas en bánda.
Sheets (to sail with flowing), navegár á escóta lárga.
Shell, cája de motón.
Shift (to), trasluchár, túmbar.
Shift a berth (to), mudár fóndo.
Shift a tackle (to), enmendár un aparéjo.
Shift the sails (to), cambiár las vélas.
Shift the helm (to), cambiár el timón.
Shift the royal (to), depasár el ayúste.
Shift the cargo (to), volvér la estíva.
Shift (the ballast shifts), el lástre se córre.
Shifter, ayúda de cocinéro.
Shifting, volánte.
Ship, búque, náve.
Ship a heavy sea (to), embarcár un gólpe de **mar.**
Ship (clearing of a), hacér el zafarráncho.
Ship (merchant), búque mercánte.
Ship of war, navío de guérra.
Ship of the line, navío de línea, navío de álto bórdo.
Ship (three-decked), navío de tres puéntes.
Ship (store), búque de almacén.
Ship (to), armár.
Ship (to clear a ship at the custom-house), **despachár**
    un búque en la aduána.
Ship-building yard, astilléro de construcción.
Ship-carpenter, carpintéro de ribéra.
Ship's company, equipáge.
Ship's way, camíno.
Ship's outside, bórdo.
Ship-shape, en buéna condición, bién orientádo.
Shiver, roldána.
Shiver (to), **fameár, tocár.**

Shiver a sail (to), braceár al filo.

Shoe the anchor (to), calzár el áncla.

Sholes, soléras.

Shoot (the ballast shoots), el lástre se córre.

Shore, la tiérra.

. Shore (close in), arrimádo á la tiérra.

Shore (to put on), metér á tiérra.

Shore (to), escorár.

Shore-anchor, áncla de pláya.

Shoulder of mutton sail, guáira.

Shove (to), desfondár.

Shrouds, obénques.

Shrouds (bowsprit), mostáchos del bauprés.

Shrouds (bumkin), pié de servioléta.

Shrouds (futtock), arraigádas.

Shrouds (main), obénques mayóres.

Shrouds (main-topgallant), obenquítos del juanéte mayór.

Shrouds (preventer), obénques volántes.

Shrouds (to ease the), largár los obénques.

Side, amuráda, bánda, bórdo, costádo.

Side of the waist, amuráda del cómbes.

Side wind, viénto á la cuádra, viénto al través.

Side (lee), costado de sotavénto.

Side (starboard), banda de estribór.

. Side (weather), costado de barlovento.

Side-rope (awning), nérvio del tóldo.

Signal flag, bandéra de señáles.

Signals (fog), señales de brúma.

Single, single.

Single-made, enterízo.

Single mast, masteléro enterízo.

Sink (to sink or to founder), afondár, ír á píque.

Sir-marks, púntas de bagáras.

Sister-blocks, motónes herrádos.

Size, ména.

Skeeds or Skids, baradéros.

Skegg, remáte de la quílla.

Skiff, esquífe.

Skim the ocean (to), peinár las ólas.

Skin, camiséta.

Skipper, maéstro de embarcación.

Skylight, lumbréra.

Skysail, montéra.

Sky-scrapers, rascanúbes, rascaciélos.

Slab-line, briolín.

Slack, séno, sobrancéro, pendúra, pandéo, en bánda.

Slack ropes, cábos suéltos ó en bánda.

Slack-cloth, embebído.

Slack-sail, véla faldóna.

Slack ship, búque pesádo.

Slatch, el medío de un cabo suélto.

Slatch of fine weather, moménto de buén tiémpo.

Sleeper, cúrva de yúgo.

Sliding-guntersail, véla guáira.

Sling, salvácha, eslínga.

Sling of a yard, estróbo de vérga ó crúz de vérga.

Slings of the buoy, guarnición de la bóya.

Slip the cable (to), alargár el cáble.

Slips for launching ships, anguílas.

Sloop, balándra.

Sloop of war, corbéta.

Slope or Slopewise, biúje.

Slow ship, búque pesádo.

Slue (to), revirár.

Smack, sumáca.

Small anchor, áncla sencílla, áncla de léva.

Small xebeck, jabéga.

Snatchblock, pastéca.

Snock, husíllo, esnón.

Snother or Snotter, estróbo de pálo.
Socket of the capstan (iron), cóncha de cabrestánte.
Sole of a gun-port, batipórte inferiór.
Sole of the rudder, zapáta del timón.
Sond (to), arfár.
Sound (to), sondeár ó sondár.
Sounding (lead), sónda de escandállo.
Sounding-lead, escandállo.
Sounding-line, sondalésa.
Soundings, sóndas.
Soundings (out of), fuéra de sóndas.
Spankèr, mesána.
Spans, amántes.
Spans of the lifts, amántes de los amantíllos.
Span-rope, nérvio.
Span-shackle, súncho ó cépo del pescánte del áncla.
Spar, berlínga, pércha, bordón.
Spare, repuésto.
Spare deck, crujía.
Spare masts, madéra de respéto.
Spare stores, pertréchos de respéto.
Spear (pump), ásta de bómba.
Spear-box, guarnición de bómba.
Speed (the), el andár.
Spell the pump (to), rendír los marinéros a la bómba.
Spell the watch (to), llamár á la guárdia.
Spend a mast (to), perdér un pálo.
Spencer-mast, husíllo, esnón.
Spencer (fore), trinquéte cangréjo.
Spike (marling), pasadór.
Spikes, clávos.
Spiles, clavíllos.
Spill (to), braceár al filo, apagár.
Spilling-lines, trápas de las vélas, apagavélas.
Spindle of the vane, húso, fiérro de la grímpola.

Spindle of the capstan, pínola del cabrestánte.

Spindle of the steering-wheel, máza de la ruéda del timón.

Spirketing, cosedéros ó sobretrancaníles.

Splice (to), ayustár, hacér costúra.

Splice, costúra de cábo.

Splice (eye), costúra de ójo, gáza.

Splice (earing), ójo.

Splice (long), costúra lárga ó españóla.

Splice (to bend with a), ajustár con costúra.

Splice (short), costúra córta ó flaménca.

Splicing-fid, burél, pasadór.

Split (to), rifárse.

Spoon (to), navegár a dos púños.

Spoondrift, rocío del mar.

Spread (the), ábra.

Spring (to), rendír un pálo ó vérga.

Spring, tangidéra, barlóa.

Spring a leak (to), hacér água.

Spring a butt (to), soltárse el estrémo de un tablón.

Spring-stay, contra estái.

Spring-tide, maréa víva.

Sprit, vérga aparéjo de abaníco, botavára, ásta.

Spritsail, cebadéra, véla de abaníco.

Spritsail-braces, bázos de cebadéra.

Spritsail-yard, vérga de cebadéra.

Sprit-topsail, sobrecebadéra.

Spunyarn, meollár.

Spurs of the beams, pernádas de los báos.

Spurs of the bits, cúrvas de las bítas.

Squall, fugáda, viénto repentíno.

Squall (southerly), fugáda solána.

Squall (violent), rafága.

Squall with rain, chubásco, borrásca.

Squally, chubascóso, borrascóso.

Square, cuádra.

Square the yards (to), braceár en crúz, ponér las vérgas en crúz.

Squareyard, vérga redónda.

Square-cloth, páño cuadrádo.

Square-rigged, aparéjo redóndo ó de cruzámen.

Square-timbers, madéros, escuadrádos.

Staff, ásta.

Staff (ensign), ásta de bandéra de pópa.

Staff (flag), ásta de tópe.

Staff (jack), ásta de bandéra de próa.

Stage (floating), pláncha de água.

Stage (hanging), pláncha de viénto.

Stanchions, puntáles.

Stanchions (awning), candeléros del tóldo.

Stanchions of the entering-ropes, candeléros del portalón.

Stanchions (poop-lantern), arcobotánte del faról de pópa

Stanchions (quarter), candeléros ó grampónes.

Stand (to), velár.

Stand by the halliards (to), velár la dríza.

Stand in-shore (to), corrér para la tiérra.

Stand off (to), tenérse léjos, salír de tiérra.

Stand on the same tack (to), corrér del mísmo bórdo.

Standard, cúrva capuchína.

Standard (royal), estandárte reál.

Standing-jib, fóque principál.

Standing part, caída de una bandéra.

Standing rigging, manióbra firme, járcia muérta.

Standing ropes, járcia muérta.

Starboard, estribór.

Start (the), arrancáda.

Staunch, sáno de quílla y costádos.

Stay, gratíl, nérvio, estái ó estáy.

Stay a ship (to), arribár.

Stay (bob), freníllo.
Stay (fore), estái de trinquéte.
Stay (foretop), estái de velácho.
Stay (fore-topgallant), estái de juanéte de próa.
Stay (flagstaff), estái de galópe ó de cabéza.
Stay (jack), nérvio de una vérga.
Stay (main), estái mayór.
Stay (mizen), estái de mesána.
Stay (maintop), estái de gávia ó estái del masteléro mayór.
Stay (mizentop), estái de sobremesána.
Stay (main-topgallant), estái de juanéte mayór.
Stay(mizen-topgallant),estái de juanéte de sobremesána
Stay (preventer), estái fálso, contraestái.
Stay (royal), estái de sobrejuanéte.
Stay (shifting), estái volánte.
Stay-gore, brúsca del gratíl.
Stays (back), brandáles.
Stays (heaving in), viénto á fil de róda.
Stays (to miss), faltár la viráda.
Staysail, véla de estái.
Staysail (fore), trinquetílla.
Staysail (main), véla de estái mayór.
Staysail (main-topmast), véla de estái de gávia.
Staysail (main-topgallant), véla de estái de juanéte mayór.
Staysail (middle), véla de estái volánte.
Staysail (mizen), véla de estái de mesána, matasoldádos.
Staysail (mizen-topmast), véla de estái de sobremesána
Staysail (mizen-topgallant), véla de estái de periquíto.
Staysail-sheets, escótas de las vélas de estái.
Steam and sailing vessel, búque místo.
Steamer, búque á vapór.
Steer (to), gobernár.
Steerage, rancho de la gente.

Steering-wheel, ruéda del timón.
Steersman, tímonél, timonéro.
Steeve, graduación.
Steeving, elevación demasiada del bauprés.
Stem, róda, mámparo, bránque.
Stem to stern (from), del mámparo de pópa al mámparo de próa.
Stemson, contraróda.
Step, carlínga.
Stern, pópa.
Stern (square), pópa llána, ó pópa cuadráda.
Stern wind, viénto por la pópa.
Stern-fasts, amárras de pópa, codéras.
Stern-frame, cuadérna de pópa.
Sterh-gallery, jardínes de pópa.
Stern-ports, pórtas de guardatimón.
Stern-post, codáste.
Sternway (to make), reculár.
Stevedore, estivadór.
Steward, despenséro.
Steward's room, despénsa.
Stiff ship, búque dúro ó búque de aguánte.
Still or dead waters, águas muértas.
Stirrups of the yards, estríbos de guardamancébos de las vérgas.
Stirrups of the yardarms, estríbos de los pelónes de lás vergas.
Stirrups of the chain-plates, estríbos de las cadénas.
Stitch, puntáda.
Stitch (to), apuntár.
Stitch (back), pespúnte.
Stitch (cross), púntos cruzádos, lláves.
Stitch (round), púnto de bigorrílla.
Stitch (to back), pespuntár.
Stockblocks, polínas de la gráda.

Stock, astilléro ó gráda de construcción.
Stock of an anchor, cépo de áncla.
Stools, mesétas de los jardínes.
Stopper (to), bozár.
Stopper (anchor), capón.
Stopper-bolts, argóllas de bóza.
Stoppers, bózas.
Store sails, vélas de respéto.
Store-keeper, pañoléro.
Store-room, pañól.
Store-room (boatswain's), pañól de contramaéstre.
Storm, temporál.
Storm coat, capóte.
Stormjib, fóque de cápa.
Stormsail of a lugger, tallaviénto.
Stormsail, véla de fortúna.
Storm-driver, mesána de cápa.
Storm-lateensail, pichóla.
Storm-mainsail, quechemarína, mayór de cápa.
Stow (to), estivár.
Stow in bulk (to), arrumár á búlto.
Stow the anchors (to), alotár las ánclas.
Stowage, estíva.
Strain (to), atormentár.
Strake (to heel a), tumbárse de una tráca.
Strakes, trácas ó hiládas.
Strand (heart), corazón de cábo.
Strand (to), encallár.
Strands, cordónes.
Strap or Strop, gáza de motón, estróbo de rémo.
Streamer, flámula.
Stream-anchor, anclóte.
Stream cable, calabróte.
Strengthen (to), reforzár.
Strengthening-line, batidór, nérvio de la véla latína.

Stress, avería.

Stress (to), atormentár.

Stretch (to), disparárse.

Stretch out (to), tesár.

Stretch out to sea (to), tirár á la mar.

Strike (to), arriár, calár.

Strike the topmasts (to), calár los masteléros.

Strike the sails (to), arriár las vélas.

Strike on a rock (to), escollár.

Strike the flag (to), arriár la bandéra.

Strike soundings (to), sondeár.

Striker (dolphin), móco.

String, durmiénte del alcazár y castíllo.

Strip (to), desaparejár.

Stroke's-man, patrón de bóte.

Stud-booms or Studdingsail-booms, botalónes de las álas y rastréras, tangónes.

Studdingsail-yard, vérga de ála.

Studdingsails (lower), rastréras.

Studdingsails (upper), álas.

Studdingsails (fore-topgallant), álas de juanéte de próa

Studdingsails (royal), álas de sobrejuanéte.

Stuff, betún.

Stuff (thick), tablónes.

Surf, resáca.

Surge, sálto, lascón.

Surge (to), saltár, lascár.

Survey (to), arqueár, reconocér.

Survey (the), arquéo.

Surveyor, períto, inspectór de marína.

Swab, lampázo.

Swab (to), lampaceár.

Swallow-tail scarf, escárpe, cóla de miláno.

Sway (to), halár, guindár.

Sway up the yards (to), izár las vérgas.

Sweep, curvedád.
Sweep of the foot, cóla de páto.
Sweep the bottom (to), rastreár.
Swell, agitación de la mar, mar de léva.
Swift (to), tortorár, dar tortóres.
Swifter, coróna.
Swing round (to), dar vuélta sóbre las ánclas.
Swing-boom, botalón rastréro.
Swivel-hook, gáncho giratório.

T

Table, váina, mésa.
Tabled, envainádo.
Tabled sail, véla envaináda.
Tabling, váina.
Tabling (head), váina del gratíl.
Tabling (foot), váina del pujámen.
Tabling (leech), váina de la valúma.
Tack, púño de la amúra, amúra, bórdo, bandéra de próa
Tack (main), amúra de la mayór.
Tack of a flag, amúra de una bandéra, rabíza de bandéra
Tack of a sail, amúra.
Tack (on the larboard), amurádo á babór.
Tack (on the starboard), amurádo á estribór.
Tack (to make a), hacér un bórdo.
Tack (to stand on the same), corrér sobre el mísmo bórdo
Tack (to stand on the other), cambiár de amúra.
Tack-gore, brúsca del martíllo.
Tack-tackle, aparéjo de amúra.
Tacks (fore), amúras del trinquéte.
Tacks (leeward), amúras de revés.
Tacks (preventer), contraamúras.
Tacks (to haul on board the), amurár.

Tacks (to haul on board the main), amurár la mayór.
Tacking-trim, aparéjo de bolína.
Tackle, aparéjo, cordáge, járcia.
Tackle (fore), aparéjo del trinquéte.
Tackle (jigger), lanteón.
Tackle (main or winding), aparéjo reál.
Tackle (reef), amánte de rízos.
Tackle (stay), candeletón, estrínque.
Tackle (tail), palanquín de rabíza.
Tackle-hook, gáncho de aparéjo.
Tackle-fall, tíra de aparéjo.
Taff-rail, coronamiénto.
Tail-block, motón de rabíza.
Tail-sail (ring), maricangálla, álas de cangréjo.
Tail-tackle, palanquín de rabíza.
Take (to), tomár.
Take aback (to), tomár por avánte.
Take off the bolt-rope (to), desrelingár.
Tallow, sébo.
Tally the sheet (to), cazár las escótas.
Tank, aljíbe.
Tar, alquitrán.
Tar, marinéro.
Tar-brush, escopéro, pincél.
Tarpaulin, encerádo.
Tarred-line, béta négra ó alquitranáda.
Tartan, tartána, una pequéña embarcación de úso en
    el mediterráneo.
Taunt, guínda.
Taunt-masted ship, búque de múcha guínda.
Taut (to haul), tesár.
Taut-hauled, téso.
Taut sail (a), véla lléna.
Tender, escampavía, patáche.
Tenon, mécha.

Thickstuff, tablónes, palmejáres.

Thickstuff (clamp), palmejáres de los durmiéntos.

Thickstuff (floor), palmejáres del plán.

Thickstuff (scarf), palmejáres de los escárpes.

Thimble, guardacábo.

Thimble-hook, gáncho de guardacábo.

Third jib, fóque tercéro.

Thole, toléte.

Throat, cangréja, boca.

Throat-seizing, garganteadúra.

Throat of a knee, bragáda de una cúrva.

Throat of the main-boom, bóca de botavára.

Thwart, bancáda.

Tide, maréa.

Tide (full), plenamár.

Tide (ebb), bajamár.

Tide-way, canál de la maréa.

Tides (neep), águas chífles ó muértas.

Tides (spring), águas vívas.

Tight, estánco, téso.

Tiller, cáña del timón.

Tiller-rope, guárdin de la cáña.

Tiller-hole, liméra.

Tiller-transom, descánso de la cáña del timón.

Tilt-bote, carróza.

Timber, madéra de construcción, ligazónes.

Timbers (cant), cuadérnas bájo un angúlo obtúso con la quílla.

Timbers (filling), cuadérnas de hencimiénto.

Timbers (floor), varéngas.

Timbers (head), gambótas de próa.

Timbers (stern), gambótas de pópa.

Timbers (top), revéses.

Timoneer, timonél, timonéro.

Toggle, cazonéta.

Ton, toneláda, iguál á 2240 lbs. ó 1016 kilógramaн.

Tonnage, toneláje, pórte.

Top, sombréro, tópe, cófa.

Top a yard (to), amantillár una vérga.

Top (fore), cófa de trinquéte.

Top (main), cófa mayór.

Top (mizen), cófa de mesána.

Topgallantmast-crosstrees, crucétas.

Topgallantsail (mizen), periquíto.

Topgallant-staysail (main), véla estái de juanéte mayór

Topgallant-staysail (mizen), véla de estái de periquíto.

Topgallant-yard (main), vérga de juanéte mayór.

Topgallant-yard (fore), vérga de juanéte de próa.

Topgallant-yard (mizen), vérga de juanete de sobremesána.

Topgallantsail (gaff), sobreescandalósa.

Topgallantsail, juanéte.

Topgallantsail (main), juanéte mayór.

Topgallantsail (fore), juanéte de próa.

Topgallantsail (mizen), juanéte de sobremesána.

Topgallantsail (flying), juanéte volánte.

Topmast, masteléro.

Topmast-staysail (main), véla de estái ne gávia.

Topmast-staysail (mizen), véla de estái de sobremesána

Top-armour, empavesádas de las cófas.

Top-block, motón de viradór.

Top-chain, estróbo de vérga.

Top-cloth, batidéro.

Top-lantern, faról de cófa.

Top-lining, batidéro.

Top-man, gaviéro.

Top-rails, batayólas de las cófas.

Top-rigging encapilladúra.

Top-rope, amánte de viradór, ó viradór.

Top-tackle, aparéjo de viradór.

Topped (high), alteróso.
Topping-lifts, amantíllos de la botavára.
Topsail (fore), velácho.
Topsail (main), gávia.
Topsail (save all), gávia volánte.
Topsail (to), guindár.
Topsail-sheets, escotínes.
Topsail-yard (main), vérga de gávia.
Topsail-yard (mizen), vérga de sobremesána.
Topsails, gávias.
Topsails (main and), aparéjo principál.
Topsails set (to have the), tenér las gávias lárgas.
Topsails (to back the), ponér las gávias en fácha.
Total amount of the gore, brúsca totál.
Touch at a port (to), tocár, hacér escála en un puérto.
Touch the wind (to), ceñír.
Tow, atoáge ó espía.
Tow (to), remolcár ó tomár á remólque.
Towage, deréchos de sírga.
Tow-line, guindaléza.
Towing-path, sirguería.
Trabacolo (Austrian), trabáculo.
Tracing-line, perrigállo.
Track, estéla.
Tracker, sirguéro.
Tracking-rope, sírga.
Trackscout, traquescóte.
Tradewinds, viéntos generáles.
Transoms, yúgos.
Transoms (wing), yúgos principáles.
Transoms (deck), yúgos de la cubiérta.
Transoms (lower), yúgos inferióres.
Transoms (helmport), contrayúgos.
Transoms (hilling), yúgos de henchimiénto.
Transom-knees, coráles.

Transport, transpórte.

Tree (axle), óje.

Trees (trestle), báos reáles de las cófas.

Trench the ballast, separár el lástre con mámparos.

Trend (to), hacér gran fuérza de véla.

Trim (to), mareár, estivár, abarrotár.

Trim a sail (to), orientár,

Trim a sheet (to), cazár.

Trim sharp up, or by the wind (to), braceár á ceñír.

Trim the sheet (to), enjuncár, hacér el enjúnque.

Trim down a sheet (to), arranchár.

Trim (in good), en buénas águas, en buéna disposición.

Trim the hold, abarrotár.

Trimming, orientación, equilíbrio.

Trimmed by the head or stern, aproádo.

Tringuard, trincádo.

Trip (to), zarpár.

Triving-line, perigállo.

Truck, bertéllo ó vertéllo.

Truck (channel), bertéllo de canál.

Trucks of the shrouds, bertéllos de los obénques.

Trucks of the vane-spindles, bólas de las grímpolas.

Trucks (parrel), vertéllos del racaménto.

Truss, trocéo, tróza ó bastárdo.

Try (to), capeár.

Try under bare poles (to), capeár á la bretóna ó á pálos sécos.

Trying, á la cápa.

Trysail-mast, esnón.

Trysail (mizen), mesána de cápa.

Trysail, véla de fortúna.

Tug or Towing-boat, remolcadór.

Tumbling-sided ship, búque abiérto de bócas.

Turn away (to), arribár.

Turn the head of a ship, aproár.

Turn of the cable round the bits, abitadúra.
Turn-table, mésa giratória.
Turned-clue, púño de gáza.
Twist (to), corchár.
Twisting, córcha.
Twisting (to lash with), atortorár.
Tye, amánte, óstaga.
Tye (topsail), óstaga de gávia.
Tye (false), béza de óstaga.

U

Unballast (to), delastrár.
Unbend (to), desenvergár.
Unbend the anchor (to), desentalingár el áncla.
Unbit (to), desabitár.
Undecked, abiérto.
Under bare poles (to be), corrér.
Under sail, á la véla.
Unfurl a sail (to), largár ó desaferrár una véla.
Unhang the tiller (to), desmontár lo cáña del timón.
Unlace (to), descosér.
Unmast (to), desarbolár.
Unmoor (to),desamarrár, desaferrár, levantár las ánclas
Unrope (to), desrelingár.
Unrig (to), desaparejár.
Unship (to), desembarcár, desmontár.
Untarred rope, cábo blánco.
Untight, en bánda.
Untwist (to), descorchár.
Up, arríba.
Upper deck, cubiérta tercéra.
Upper sails, vélas áltas.
Upper-work, óbra muérta.

Upper work of a ship, acastilláje.
Upright, en candéla.
Upset (to), zozobrár.

V

Valances, cenéfas.
Vane, grímpola.
Vane (dog), cataviénto.
Vane-spindle, húso ó hiérro de la grímpola.
Vane-stock, armazón de la grímpola.
Vangs, óstas, búrras de mesána.
Veer (to), birár ó virár.
Veer and haul (to), lascár y halár.
Veering about, viráda.
Ventilator, manguéra.
Vessel, búque, bárco, bajél, embarcación, navío.
Vessel (revenue), guardacóstas.

W

Waist, cómbes, crujía.
Waist-cloths, empavesádas.
Wake, águas, estéla, remolínos del timón.
Wale, cínta.
Wale (chain), mésa de guarnición.
Wale (channel), cínta de la segúnda cubiérta.
Wale (gun), Regála.
Wale (main), cínta principál ó mayór.
Wall-knot, píña.
Warp, urdído, urdímbre, espía, calabróte, entalingádo.
Warrant-officers, oficiáles subaltérnos de mar.
Watch, guárdia, singladúra.
Watch-glasses, ampollétas.

Watch (dog), segúnda guárdia.
Watch (to set the), rendír la guárdia.
Watch (to spell the), llamár la guárdia.
Water (dead), águas.
Water-tight, estánco, á pruéva de água.
Water-line (load), línea de água de cárga.
Water-line, línea de água.
Water-logged, anegádo en el água.
Water-sail, arrastracúlo, rastréra.
Water-ways, trancaníles.
Watering-boat, aljíbe.
Way, camíno.
Way (to get under), salír, principiár viáge.
Weather or Waist-boards, fálcas.
Weather (to), montár ó doblár, barloventeár.
Weather (hard-a), metér tódo á barlovénto.
Weather-arm, cár.
Weather-cloth, tóldo de inviérno.
Weather-gage, barlovénto ó lóf.
Weather-side, costádo de barlovénto.
Weather-shore, cósta de barlovénto.
Weather-sheets, escótas de barlovénto.
Weft, tráma.
Well, árca de bómba.
Wheel (steering), ruéda del timón.
Wheel-ropes, guardínes.
Wherry, barquílla, bóte de pasáje.
Whip-staff, pinzóte del timón.
Winch, cigueñál.
Wind, viénto.
Wind aft, viénto en pópa.
Wind and water (between), á flór de água.
Wind a call (to), tocár el píto.
Wind a ship (to), cambiár la próa.
Wind on the beam, viénto derrotéro.

Wind right ahead, viénto á fil de róda.
Wind (bow), viénto por la amúra.
Wind (head or ahead), viénto por la próa.
Wind (fair), viénto favoráble.
Wind (large or leading), viénto lárgo.
Wind (quarterly), viénto por la aléta.
Wind (side), viénto á la cuádra, viénto al través.
Wind (stern), viénto por la pópa.
Wind (sharp), viénto de bolína.
Wind (steady), viénto hécho.
Wind (to), birár ó virár.
Wind (to come or haul to the), orzár.
Wind (to keep to the), orzár tódo.
Wind (to sail by, abreast of, or on the), navegár
    con viénto de través.
Wind (to sail before the), navegár en pópa.
Wind (to fly up to the), partír al púño.
Wind (violent), bríza carabinéra.
Wind-bound, detenído por viéntos contrários.
Wind-taut, tumbádo al viénto.
Winding-tackle, aparéjo reál ó de estréllas.
Windlass, molinéte.
Windlass (Spanish), pálo de tortór.
Wind's eye, orígen del viénto.
Winds (baffling), ventolínas.
Winds (land), terráles.
Winds (south-western), vendaváles.
Winds (trade), viéntos genérales.
Windsail, manguéra, ventiladór.
Wing-transom, yúgo principál.
Wood or Dunnage (fathom), léña de estíva.
Woodings, cábos del tablazón.
Woold (to), trincár.
Wooldings or Wouldings, engénias, reátas.
Work (to), maniobrár.

Work (close or small long), púnto de telár.
Work (dead or upper), óbra muérta.
Work (long), púnto de váina.
Work (quick), óbra víva.
Work to windward (to), barloventeár.
Worm (to), embutír, entrañár.
Worm-eaten, abromádo.
Worming, embutidúra.
Wreck, búque naufragiádo.

X

Xebec, jabéque, una pequéña embarcación de tres pálos usáda en el mediterráneo.

Y

Yard, astilléro, vérga.
Yard (cross-jack), vérga séca ó vérga de gáta.
Yard (fore), vérga de trinquéte.
Yard (main), vérga mayór.
Yard (fore-topsail), vérga de vélácho.
Yard (main-topsail), vérga de gávia.
Yard (mizen-topsail), vérga de sobremesána.
Yard (fore-royal), vérga de sobrejuanéte de próa.
Yard (main-royal), vérga de sobrejuanéte mayór.
Yard (mizen-royal), vérga de sobreperiquíto.
Yard (fore-topgallant), vérga de juanéte de próa.
Yard (main-topgallant), vérga de juanéte mayór.
Yard (mizen-topgallant), vérga de juanéte de sobre-
    mesána.
Yard (spritsail), vérga de cebadéra.
Yard (studdingsail), vérga de ála.

Yards (square), vérgas redóndas.
Yards (to top the), amantillár las vérgas.
Yards (to square the), ponér las vérgas en crúz.
Yards (to brace the), braceár las vérgas.
Yard-arm, peñól de vérga.
Yard-tackle, aparéjo de peñól.
Yarn, meollár, filástica.
Yarn (spun or rope), meollár, filástica.
Yaw (to), guiñár.
Yawing, guiñáda.
Yawl, bóte tercér, canóa, seréni.
Yeoman, pañoléro.
Yeoman (boatswain's), pañoléro del pañól de próa.

LIVERPOOL:
PRINTED BY ROCKLIFF BROTHERS, CASTLE STREET.

LIBROS ESPAÑOLES

EN VENTA EN EL ESTABLECIMIENTO DE LOS

Señores ROCKLIFF BROTHERS,

44 CASTLE STREET, LIVERPOOL.

———————▶•◀———————

LIBROS DE CONVERSACION en ingles y español, 1/-.

DICCIONARIOS ingles y español, español é ingles, 5/6. 12/- y 24/-.

GRAMATICA INGLESA, en veinte y dos lecciones, por URCILLA, 4/-.

OLLENDORF, método para aprender el ingles, y clave, 5/-.

LIBROS DE CARGA, 1/-.

CUADERNOS DE BITACORA, 2/- á 7/-.

DIARIOS DE NAVEGACION, 3/- á 9/-.

TABLAS de THOMPSON, en ingles, 12/-.

LIBROS PARA CUBICAR, 7/6.

TABLAS DE REDUCCION del peso ingles á Kilogramos, 1/-

LIBROS RAYADOS Y EN BLANCO para cuentas.

PAPELERIA Y TINTAS de todas clases.

LIBROS PARA COPIAR CARTAS á mano y con prensa.

PRENSAS DE TODAS CLASES Y TAMAÑOS.